Ordinary GI

An ordinary draftee in World War II

By
Gordon C. Krantz

COVER:
Bailey Bridge, the "assemble-on-site" bridge
of the Author's Engineer company
diagrammed,
and the Author
in 1944

ISBN: 978-0-6152-1047-6

Author: gnrkrantz@aol.com
Also available from: lulu.com

Table of CONTENTS

Chapter	**Page**
The Setting: World War II	1
Drafted	3
Inducted	5
Basic Training	9
Maneuvers	25
Oklahoma Interlude	33
To Europe on the Liz	37
England	41
Across France: the Great Rat Race ...	47
Stalemate at the West Wall	77
Luxembourg	99
Germany	115
Southern France	141
Discharged!	151
Looking Back	153

The Setting: World War II

The war was a total war. No one was a bystander; everyone was in the war in some way. My military service was just one part of that.

Civilians were in the war with both feet. There was rationing, naturally. You might have had the money to buy sugar or meat, but you couldn't buy it if you didn't have any more ration coupons for it. You could get only so many gallons of gasoline per month, you could buy only so much meat, you could get only one new tire per year.

Civilians saved used cooking fat for munitions. We cut both ends out of tin cans, put the ends inside, and flattened the can for salvage. People combed the woods for discarded scrap metal. Everyone worked and women entered the work force in unprecedented numbers.

Many years from now, if there are archaeologists digging in the garbage dumps of the Twentieth Century, they'll come across the normal progression of trash until they encounter a layer dated to the early 1940s with no tin cans and almost no other metals. Unless they have a written history to consult they'll be at loss to explain this strange layer. You didn't throw away metal. It was important.

At any rate, World War II was a total war. Some of us served in uniform. The rest served in civilian clothes.

The war was not as much in doubt by mid-1943 as it had been at the beginning but we were by no means certain that the US would win. We had been at war for a year and a half when I was inducted and although the European fronts had stabilized, the Pacific was still iffy.

Everyone who was male and breathing expected to go into the armed forces. It was natural—taken for granted, accepted, even embraced. Those of us who had been following the news knew that the world was at stake.

1

There was no glamour to it, either. The war that had taken the glamour out of fighting, World War I, had been over for only 23 years. So little time of unsettled peace, with the Spanish civil war and the Japanese invasion of China marring even that peace and, starting in the late 1930s, totalitarian aggression in Europe and Ethiopia.

Well, there was the Great Depression, too. But that's a different story. Looking back, I think that the Depression was the best preparation we could have had to face a war. We already knew how to do without, to make do, to wear out, and to repair.

The casualty reports in the news were specific. There was no sugar coating. Most of it was along the lines of Churchill's "blood, toil, sweat, and tears." Duty was a powerful organizer of one's thinking in those days. For some of us, it still is.

That was the climate in which I went into the war.

You're used to reading the stories of heroes and stories about great battle trials and suffering. You won't find this to be the story of a hero, but of an ordinary GI.

As you read this journal you may be struck, as I was, by the fact that I had it pretty easy in the war. I certainly wasn't a hero nor did I have to fight all the time. That was the fate of the Infantry, and I was a Light Ponton (not "*pontoon!*") Engineer. Besides, I always seemed to get the soft jobs even within our Company. At a Company reunion many years later I asked the First Sergeant why it was that I got off with the best assignments. He said, "Don't ask me, ask the Company Clerk. I gave all that stuff to him." Super (we all went by just our last names) the Company Clerk said that he didn't remember anything like that. So I guess that my gratitude goes where it belongs, to God.

Drafted

In the fall of 1942, after graduating from high school, I began to attend the Bethel Junior College in St. Paul. I don't remember all of how I afforded college but I had worked as a fettler at the Red Wing Potteries that summer for the going wage of 52¢ an hour.

> *A fettler is the guy who scrapes the dry glaze from the bottoms and lid-rims of things like cookie jars so that they won't stick to the kiln car when they're fired and the glaze melts.*

> *(Later in this story you'll find more of these italicized inset paragraphs. Most of them are reports of follow-up visits to Europe in the 1970s to 1990s I could have used footnotes, but some of them would be too long.)*

Anyhow, college was my first real time away from home. I was a green farm boy and I needed to get off the farm for a while. I was as much of a hick as anyone could be, except that I was an eccentric one: I had read every encyclopedia I could find, I had a fossil collection, I wrote stuff. Even after four years of high school in the big city (Red Wing, population 10,000) I was just about totally inadequate socially, but people seemed to like me. Even girls, but I had no idea of what to do about that. I was a shy hick. I didn't have a date until after the war.

As a college student, I was a possible candidate for officer training. There was a program, I think named V12, in which you could get college support in return for entering the Navy for three years. I took the tests and passed. Then came the physical, and bad teeth barred me. It turned out to be just as well. I would have made a terrible officer, even in the Navy.

So in about November 1942 I checked with my draft board. When would I be called? About April, they said. That told me that I could finish the first semester of my freshman college year, but not the second semester. The war manpower situation was such that there were no student deferments.   On the strength of that information I wound up my college in early January, didn't register for the second semester, and went back to Red Wing to await the call.

I think that that was about the time I took a job in the Red Wing Sewer Pipe factory. My job was to take wet sections of clay pipe off the platform of the extruder. The sections were eight inches across and a couple of feet long. Then I was to swing sideways and stack them on the cart that would take them away to be dried. Holding a fairly heavy weight in front of the body and pivoting is exactly what will crush a spinal disk, and in a day and a half it did just that. I went home and spent a week or so in bed. None of us had heard of workers' compensation, and I guess it wasn't yet a law. But that disk has pursued me all my life. The Army didn't find it when they inducted me, and I haven't really been crippled by it (wore a body brace for three years in the late '40s, though), so we'll consider it a footnote only.

I waited for the draft call. March, no notice. April, no notice. I went to the draft board, and was told that I would probably be called in the summer. Look, I said, I quit college to be drafted. Wait, they said, maybe May. I took a job at a local nursery.

May, no notice. I went to the draft board and tried to enlist. They wouldn't take me. The manpower situation was so tight that they had to control the flow of draftees. No enlistments allowed.

In June came the letter from the Draft Board:

"The President of the United States, to Gordon C. Krantz: Greetings.

You have been selected by a committee of your friends and neighbors ..."

Inducted

The armed services had a well-oiled set of procedures for induction in place by then. I suppose that it was for the sake of efficiency that we were called up in groups. The group of inductees from the Red Wing area on July 6, 1943 was large, maybe a couple dozen, duly recorded by a group picture in the local newspaper.

We were all sworn in and shipped to Fort Snelling. At that time the Fort was larger, and the parade ground and barracks spilled over onto what is now part of the airport. Air travel was uncommon in those days and the Wold Chamberlain Airport (its name before it became the Minneapolis-Saint Paul International Airport) was invisible to us. The biggest plane then landing and taking off was the DC-3, known as the C-47 in its military guise. I don't recall hearing any planes there.

A "company" at the induction center was made up of whoever had just come in from around Minnesota, western Wisconsin, the eastern Dakotas, and northern Iowa. Turning us into soldiers began immediately.

We were under the command of a Master Sergeant, and he was as tough as an old he-goat. His job was to keep us so busy hating him that we wouldn't notice how we were being sweated out. His voice and language were coarse and loud. We learned how to stand straight and look straight ahead while he cruised and badgered us. When we took a break and sat down, in the shade if there was any, he had us sing Army songs, and he'd profanely chew the hide off anyone who didn't sing loud enough. Tone deafness was no excuse. Of course, it was a bit hard on those of us who were conservative Christian, and who had difficulty with the mild profanity of Army songs. We mumbled.

We thought that July on the Fort Snelling parade ground was blistering hot. Little did we know about hot then.

We spent only about two weeks at Fort Snelling, being shaped into instant responders and learning how to avoid being "volunteered" for duties like KP.

> *KP or Kitchen Police. The work is no harder than drilling, but the guard rousts you out of bed at 5 AM and you go to get yelled at by the Mess Sergeant. The Mess Sergeant is pretty much like the cartoon characters you see as Head Chefs in television shows. They are driven, so they drive you. For that day, they own you. No one wants to be on KP. It's undignified.*

We got basic marching drill and some instruction in weapons. Mostly, we got used to getting up and getting into formation exactly on time, and getting to bed and shutting up on time, too. All together. This is called "the Army routine."

Then about a hundred of us were herded together and put on a train. They trucked us to the old St. Paul Union Depot, the biggest building I'd been in. We were going to Texas, they said. None of us had been more than a hundred miles from home before, and this was "it."

The train was an adventure. My first train ride, I believe. We had by now learned to take whatever someone had decided for us, and to just go along and hunker down when necessary and take evasive action when necessary. Someone else made our decisions.

We got to Kansas City and changed trains. We were there only a few hours, but we got out and stretched. As I recall, it was up to us to get back onto the train when we were supposed to, because we wandered off on our own.

There is a hill across the street from the Kansas City train station, and on top was a World War I memorial. More to my taste, the hill was dry and not well lawned, so that the bones of the hill showed through. I promptly found a handful of fossils, mostly brachiopods and bryozoans. Still have them. The day wasn't wasted. I have no idea what the other guys did.

> *Last time I was in Kansas City, the train station was still there, but the surrounding area had been transformed. No more fossil hunting.*

Then back on the train. It's a long way to Texas by train. The one scene that persists in my retina is looking back from what seems to have been the last car and seeing the straight rails converge and disappear on the horizon through the dead flat, hot, brown Kansas wasteland. Though there were sunflowers.

Basic Training

Basic Training is a process designed to wring out the last traces of civilian-ism and to create a soldier. Let me shift to the present tense now, because it's still so vivid. No one forgets Basic Training.

We arrive in Texas on July 14, and the temperature is 114 in the shade, and there is no shade. We are immediately fallen in for a five-mile hike with full packs. You make that hike, and you can take the rest OK. I make it half way and collapse beside the road. When half the Company has gone by I get up and struggle back to my place in the lead platoon. I have begun to become a soldier.

We have been deposited at Camp Howze. The camp is beside the north-south highway just south of the Red River that forms the boundary between Texas and Oklahoma, and it is a few miles out of the city of Gainsville.

> *Interstate 35 has since replaced the highway past Camp Howze. When I drove that road in 1977 there was no trace of Camp Howze visible, but veterans from our company tell me that you can still find stubs of barrack foundations in the field.*

The Rainbow Division is there, reconstituting from inter-war shut-down. For that matter, our company is doing the same thing. We are now the 537th Engineer Light Ponton Company. It had been inactivated in the 1920s, and now is recommissioned.

A Light Ponton company (that spelling is correct—it isn't "pontoon," nor is it pronounced with an "oo;" it's "PON-t'n") a Light Ponton Company is a fairly small unit, necessarily mobile because it has the job of building temporary bridges and supplying assault boats and foot bridges for Infantry crossings of rivers. Compared to other Engineer units, an LP company is quite specialized in its role and it is held in reserve for those few and nasty times when a river has to be crossed. Within the company, personal roles are not as highly specialized as that of the Company, though there are specialists. At a bridge site the men are somewhat interchangeable. All are trained as general Engineers, being expected to be able to blow up a bridge as well as to build one. Even the cooks.

There are about 200 of us. Half is the contingent from Fort Snelling; half is a similar contingent from Fort Leonard Wood in Missouri. This makes for a much more homogeneous company than if it had been assembled from all over the country. Though we range from the jackpine savages of northern Minnesota to the hillbillies from the Ozarks of Missouri we will become a single family over the next two and a half years.

The Company is made of four platoons and each platoon is made of four rows (squads) of men. Our company commander is a First Lieutenant, Lt. Maraska. Each platoon has a Second Lieutenant and a Sergeant, and each squad has a Corporal. That is, we will have those Corporals and other Sergeants later, but as we start out we have been given some Sergeants: our cadre.

This cadre is a small group of men, most of whom served together in Panama and whose job it is to form a company. They are our four Platoon Sergeants, plus some operating administrators: a First Sergeant who runs the personnel affairs, a Master Sergeant who runs line affairs, a Supply Sergeant, and a Mess Sergeant. There is also a Motor Pool Sergeant, because we have or will have 75 vehicles. The cadre really runs the company at the first. Officers are new to the job and are supposed to be more concerned with strategy and to act through the non-commissioned officers.

The cadre covers a range of toughness but most are quite tough. They leak stories about each other. Sergeant. Osborne, for example. In Panama, they were working on a bridge in the jungle. Osborne saw a bushmaster (a very large, very poisonous snake) about to strike one of the others. He drew his .45 and shot the head off the snake. There is a limit to his toughness, though. Early on, I am using rubbing alcohol as an after-shave lotion. He is shaving next to me and asks to borrow some. Now, 70% isopropyl is not a gentle liquid. He splashes it on, and he yells as it bites into his scraped skin. This is strategic thing to do to your Platoon Sergeant because the Army is like a bunch of sharks: weakness invites attack, and now I have established myself as a tough hombre who uses raw alcohol for aftershave.

No one is as tough as the Master Sergeant, Billy Lazarr. He owns you and you both know it.

Basic training is like Fort Snelling was, only more so. We drill in the sun until we can move as a unit. A couple of our men have no sense of rhythm and always get out of step. The command then is "Everybody except (...those who were there will fill in the name); Change Step—Harch!" We take turns drilling our platoons, the Army's method of finding out who is a potential Corporal. I am not a potential anything by this test. I am good at marching the men into the side of a building while I try to figure out what the next command should be.

We get our rifles, most of them Enfields and a few Springfields. These are obsolete weapons from 1918. They fire the same ammunition as does the new M-1 rifle but they're bolt operated instead of semi-automatic. They weigh nine pounds each. We learn to disassemble them and to clean them. I draw one whose previous owners allowed rust to pit the barrel, so I can never get it to look right for inspection. I also draw a lot of KP and latrine duty in consequence. But if the inspecting Sergeant or Lieutenant wants to find a flaw, he will: a trace of oil in the chamber, perhaps. There have to be a certain number of men on KP.

On KP we learn how to peel potatoes. The knives are not very sharp. If we cut the peelings too thick, the Mess Sergeant yells, "I'll make you peel the peelings!" and he means it. KP starts just after 5 AM and lasts until the supper dishes are done and the mess hall is clean.

We learn the manual of arms. Starting with the rifle grounded, at Attention; to Port Arms; to Present Arms; to Right Shoulder Arms; to Left Shoulder Arms; to Port Arms; to Inspection Arms (rip open the bolt, snap your eyes down to verify an empty chamber, slam the bolt closed, pull the trigger); to Right Shoulder **Arms**; to Order Arms (rifle butt on the ground); back to Attention. All in unison, in rhythm.

We learn to aim the rifles. The rifle is sandbagged to hold it steady and we guide another soldier holding a pencil point on a target until it's at the point of aim, then we repeat the aim. This promotes consistency of aim. The later sighting-in will make the aim and impact coincide. At least, that's the theory.

We learn to make our beds exactly, to pack and lay out our backpacks exactly, to keep our footlockers exactly, to stand inspection of these things exactly and repeatedly. All with the threat of KP or latrine duty for failure. A well made bed is supposed to be tight enough to bounce a nickel on its middle, and the corners of the blankets are exactly 45 degrees.

We learn our serial numbers. We have to be able to recite them if we are awakened in the middle of the night with a Sergeant holding our dogtags to verify them. The number becomes indelible, so that any man will be able to recite it on command to the end of his life. "Krantz, Gordon C.! Private! 3-7-5-6-9-4-5-0!"

> *For those who don't know: dogtags are the two metal tags on a bead chain that you wear around your neck at all times, even in bed. They have your name, serial number, blood type and religious denomination. They're to identify your body, comforting thought.*

We learn proper Army forms of address. Early on, I ask my Platoon Sergeant a question, and end with "...Sir."

Sgt. Osborne rears up to a height of eight feet, leans over my face and roars that only officers are addressed as "Sir." In a voice that seems strangely level to me I respond, "I understand, Sergeant." Then I calmly repeat the question, Sgt. Osborne resumes his six-foot height, and the conversation goes on.

We learn that the draftee generation is broad. About half of our men are younger than I, and I've just turned 19. A few of the men are old – Pop Colstrum of Red Wing is at least in his thirties, and Cornell is not far behind him. In honor of his age, I guess, Pop becomes the company mailman. Sage from Kansas is almost as old as Stiff, who's maybe 30. Sage is a barber, and continues his trade in the Army. He gives me my first non-homemade haircuts.

We learn that the Army, officially segregated racially, is still somewhat integrated. "Chief" Dolson of northern Minnesota is Chippewa, and comes by his nickname honestly; his family is actually among the leadership of his band. Monroe is nominally Cherokee, but he's no doubt mixed because he's pretty black. Neither man is in any way different from those of us who are officially white, and there isn't a trace of racism from even our Southern contingent as far as those two men are concerned.

We learn to march under full pack in the Texas sun. We learn to drink water drawn into our aluminum canteens from a big rubber bag on a sling (the Lister bag, an olive drab udder) and to relish the taste of chlorine, rubber, and aluminum. We learn to conserve our water on a long, hot march.

We learn to crawl. We learn to squirm along, heads down and with rifle cradled in our elbows under barbed wire and under live machine gun bullets just overhead. We hear the story of the rookie who stood up when he met a rattlesnake. I win the bet that I can find a fossil on this, the infiltration course.

(Another "urban legend" of the infiltration course: the broken guide rail. Under the water jacket of the machine gun -- under the barrel -- is a horizontal rail that keeps the gun from firing too low as it is traversed across the course. The story is that one day the rail broke, and the gunner wiped out a whole squad before he could get his finger off the trigger. This story, and the one about the rattlesnake, are no doubt a deliberate ploy to make sure we don't stand up and that we give the bullets proper respect. Most of us don't need this added incentive to keep low.)

We learn the texture of North Texas "soil." Farmers grow cotton next to the base, so there must be some soil. All we see, and crawl over, is dry, scabrous, dusty fossil oyster beds. On the bright side, I find one fossil oyster with a fossil pearl. On the dull side, I find that pearls fossilize into the same worthless limestone as do the shells.

We learn that life is tough for non-humans also in this part of Texas. On one of our drill fields – real rough fields, not mowed parade grounds -- I find the shell of a box tortoise that seems to have died of sheer climate and send it home. I also pick up a buffalo burr, like a sand burr but with longer spikes, in my hand and have to go to the base hospital for minor surgery. The infection is bad enough so that I get a general anesthetic, the new sodium pentothal.

We learn how pleasant, in addition to attractive, Army nurses can be. I come out of the anesthetic and see another soldier getting an alcohol back rub, I demand one too, and I get it. Pentothal does that. Then they keep me for a few days, each day thrusting a curved forcep into the incision and opening it. Sulfa drugs are new, and I eat plenty of it.

We learn the dangers of "women." The Army has a series of explicit sex education films to warn us about venereal diseases and the horrors of their lesions, films that are explicit enough to make you wish for rubber gloves in order to shake hands with a girl. We learn the medico/social ritual of the short-arm inspection, when the camp doctor walks down the row of naked men standing by their foot lockers in barracks, checking for signs of venereal disease.

We learn that the Russians are good guys. All during the '30s we learned that Uncle Joe was a terrorist tyrant and that Russia was dangerous. Now, we're allies. A training film to teach us is Serge Eisenstein's great silent epic, *Alexander Nevsky*. One image from the famous battle on the ice burns into my visual cortex: the shield wall, with an axe slashing in front of it. I vaguely think of the warriors as Vikings—not far off the mark, seeing as how they were only 250 years younger than the Vikings who founded their kingdom, Rus Kiev.

> *1994: The Minnesota Orchestra plays the Prokofief score to accompany the Alexander Nevsky film. Do I go? of course, with my soon-to-be second wife Ruth. The music, live, is a lot better than the Army score. There is more to the film. I guess they cut the Army version. And the shield wall is less Viking-like. Old memories can get corrupted. Great film, though.*

We learn that some men will drink anything. One of our men is so hooked on alcohol that he'll steal witch hazel shaving lotion and drink it. And it will take half a dozen post-war years for the habit to kill him.

We learn that not everyone who passes the physical will make a soldier. One of our men is sent home on discharge because he can't stop wetting his bed. Nice guy otherwise. Medicine in 1943 isn't up to later standards.

We learn that civilian toughness is not enough. Like all farm kids I have tough feet. But on our first ten mile hike a blister under my heel sheds a 1-by-2 inch slab of leather. It will have an honored place in my display of war souvenirs.

We learn how to run while starved for air in a gas mask. These devices allow you to live on the amount of air they let through, but just barely. When you stand still the only discomfort is the hot, sweaty slab of rubber on your face. When you run, after ten steps you labor over every breath. We notice that the drill sergeant isn't wearing one while he jogs beside us. And we learn how to identify the smell of the various gases that are known then: chlorine (like bleach), mustard (a sharp smell), and phosgene (like spoiled hay). Nerve gases haven't been invented. We learn to put on a gas mask, tearing open the pouch and knocking off our helmet, and testing the seal before we take the next breath after the unexpected cry of "Gas!" Finally, we learn the value of a gas mask when we are herded into a bunker and exposed to tear gas strong enough to burn the sweaty skin around the edges of the mask.

We learn the correct technique of throwing a hand grenade (an overhand swing) and of getting down out of the way of the fragments when the pineapple explodes.

> My present display of war souvenirs includes a bunch of grenade fragments and a couple of spent firing mechanisms picked up on the range after practice. We weren't supposed to do that. I'm not a slave to rules.

We learn how to make and detonate a satchel charge. This is a bundle of dynamite sticks on a pole, with the cap and fuse properly inserted, that you're supposed to prop against an enemy firing port in a pillbox, and it's supposed to blow him up. I also learn that I absorb nitroglycerin (the active part of dynamite) through my skin and get a whomping headache every time I handle it. And we learn that dynamite gets unstable when stored, and has to be turned periodically so the nitroglycerin won't seep to the bottom and become dangerously sensitive. We dispose of our leftover dynamite in a handy pond, and the explosion sends a plume of water straight up a hundred feet. Little fish live in the shallow Texas pond and it rains fish.

We learn how to detect and how to disarm a booby trap, and how to expect one anywhere. We watch the film where a GI comes into a room and is about to sit in a chair, and thinks better of it; is about to sit on a piano bench, and reconsiders; reaches over to play the keys, and backs off; straightens a crooked picture, and the room dissolves in smoke.

> *Later, in Europe, we sometimes fail to apply this caution about booby traps. In searching a house, some of our men will take a dresser drawer and flip it over while jerking it out. We find no booby traps, fortunately.*

We learn how to locate buried mines, and how not to mess with an S-mine.

> *See the chapter about Germany for more about S-mines. Nasty things. And the foolhardy way to locate other mines. When you're young you're invulnerable. All that's later in this narrative.*

We learn how to blow up bridges as well as build them. We sit on the ground in small groups and do exercises on demolition. Although here in the States we work with dynamite, in real combat we will work with TNT, so the problems are solved in terms of half-pound blocks of TNT. We learn about tamping a charge to concentrate its force. A packing, even of mud, will increase the force of an explosion on a surface.

We learn how to calculate the amount of TNT needed to blow up a bridge. For reinforced concrete, the number of blocks is determined by the radius of rupture desired, in feet, cubed; times a constant for type of tamping; plus a percentage dependent upon reinforcement of the concrete. Sgt. Billy Lazarr describes the dimensions of a bridge abutment, then he spins on Zwak. Now, Zwak is a small, very *very* quiet farm boy from Central Minnesota, and Lazarr tends to pick on him. Lazarr snaps, "Zwak! How many blocks of TNT?" And in his quiet voice, Zwak instantly gives him the correct number. Zwak turns out to be a math whiz. We all silently cheer Zwak. We were still working on the first part of the formula. Even Lazarr tones down his hazing of Zwak after that.

We learn what real noise is. Our Company has .50 caliber machine guns assigned to it and we get to shoot them. In this exercise, the machine gun is set on a low, heavy tripod. The .50 throws 250, 2-ounce, half-inch-wide slugs per minute at 2700 feet per second, and the cartridge is nearly an inch in diameter at the butt end and eight inches long. When you fire a tracer, you can see it as a streak to the target bank some 300 yards away, and it plows through six feet of brick-hard clay and may ricochet up at an angle, to loop down a couple of miles away. A straight shot seems to hang in the air for a mile or more before it drops appreciably. The muzzle of the gun is 16 inches above the gravel of the firing pad, and after firing the gravel is beaten into concentric rings by the concussions. Even at the back of the gun you can't stand to fire more than a half dozen rounds. It feels like being in a steel barrel while a couple of railway section hands pound it with sledge hammers. We are told that, in combat, you don't mind the noise. My audiogram, six years later (and 64 years later also) will show the classic noise damage. But I love that .50, the most awesome weapon that one man can fire. That was my gun.

We learn about new weapons. I show some mechanical talent with weapons, so I'm assigned one of our four Thompson submachine guns. These are the gangster Tommy guns of the 1930s, firing clips of 25 .45 caliber pistol cartridges. They weigh 15 pounds. Along with the Thompson I find myself assigned as a jeep driver, because that's who is supposed to have that gun. I don't actually get to drive the jeep but I'm carried on the Company books as a jeep driver for a while. When the time comes to be tested on the use of our weapons I go to the Thompson range.   There, I walk along the hundred yard rough and brushy course and at irregular intervals an upper-body man-sized target flips up for about four or five seconds.   I'm to put two shots into each of the first four targets and three into the last.   I get a "possible" as my score: perfect.   As the result I get to wear an Expert badge for submachine gun.

We learn how our rifles, which we've been carrying all this time, really work.   Or don't work.   We go to the firing range and spend several days practicing.   Enfield rifles—mine is one—are bolt action and they cock on the forward stroke of the bolt.   That means that you are pushing against the firing pin spring as you push the bolt forward.   You do this while the sling is wrapped around your left arm in such a way as to threaten to pull your shoulder socket apart when you load.   And none of our rifles is accurate.   We don't do well on this.   I barely qualify.   This ain't right – at home with my little .22 you could specify which eye of a squirrel I should hit.

The drill on the range is, "Ready on the right!"   "Ready on the left!"   "Ready on the firing line!" And the Sergeant looks to see that all the guns are pointed the right direction.   A white flag goes up from the dugout behind the targets.   "The flag is waving!"   "The flag is down!" "Fire at will!"   Then the targets are pulled down and checked for holes.   And all too often, the red flag on a pole – "Maggie's drawers" -- is waved from the dugout to report no bullet holes at all.   There is banter about having a friend in the dugout with a .30 caliber pencil, just in case a hole in the target is needed.

We learn about minor health hazards of Army life. Texas is great for testing physical health.   I come down with an ingrown toenail from the marching and, more to the point, from the heat and moisture in those Army shoes.   Back to the hospital, where a third of the nail is removed.   On local anesthetic, they let me watch.   This time I can go back to the Company immediately, and draw the easy duty of latrine orderly for a couple of days.

19

We learn the Army's accommodation to religion. There is a chapel on the base and many of us attend. The services and songbooks are necessarily pretty ecumenical, although we don't know that word in the 1940s. I find that most of the songs are good Baptist fare. The sermons are generally inspirational in this homogenized "church," but chapel is a link to non-Army existence and a support in the earnestly secular world of the Army.

We learn about Army-base cities. On evening and weekend day passes we go into the "big city" of Gainsville. Some of the men overdo this and a couple who have been promoted to Corporal or Sergeant get busted down to Private again for being drunk and disorderly. Most of us simply go into town to get away from the Army.

Gainsville is quintessential Texas. I go to a restaurant on a Sunday pass, and have my first chicken-fried steak with boiled potatoes and peppered red-eye gravy. Wherever you go, you hear the tinny 1943 speakers beating out "Steel Guitar Rag," "Yellow Rose of Texas," and "Rose of San Anton'." There is really nothing to do in town except for what towns always provide to Army bases, but it's town.

We learn about "the other side." Camp Howze has a Prisoner of War stockade with German prisoners. The stockade is ringed with wire fence but no one worries much about it. From what the prisoners tell us (a surprising number -- surprising to us monolingual Americans -- speak English) their camp sure beats what they had in the German Army. Some go out on work details. Escape is not much of an option, set as they are among the barren lands of Texas. Everyone is pretty friendly about it all.

We eventually get our promotions. We have line Corporals and Sergeants, and a lot of Technical Sergeants and Corporals. The latter are the specialists, like the bulldozer operator and the motor pool mechanics. It will take me beyond the end of Basic to get my promotion, to the rank I will carry for the rest of my military service: Private First Class. It has no meaning except that I've kept my nose clean. For that, I'll also get a Good Conduct medal. Technically, Private is the lowest rank in the Army but Private First Class is its equal in reality.

We learn, or some of us learn, about other options. Toward the end of Basic I get a call to see the First Sergeant. Because of my one semester of college, and because of the scores I got on the tests given at induction, I am offered the chance to leave the Company and go to OCS, Officers Training School. I give this about seven minutes' thought and turn it down. This is a decision I will never regret. As an officer, entering my new life as a Second Lieutenant, I would most likely be assigned to an Infantry platoon. The mortality rate among such people, whether in Europe or the Pacific, is high. But the real reason for my turning it down is that by now I've bonded to my Company. We are family now.

We learn routine. Always, the assembly first thing in the morning, before breakfast. We fall out from the barracks and line up in our four platoons. Each platoon is under the command of a Sergeant and at the right end of each row of men is the squad's Corporal. An officer may walk along the rows looking for anything amiss, especially if bodies are needed for KP. Then the Corporals report, "First Squad all present and accounted for!" "Second Squad all present and accounted for!" The Sergeants call out, "Headquarters Platoon all present and accounted for!" "First Platoon (the first Bridge Platoon) all present and accounted for!" "Second Platoon all present and accounted for!" "Light Equipage Platoon all present and accounted for!" Then we fall out for breakfast.

We learn the limits of my passivity. One day my back is giving me trouble and it's complicated by a migraine. I'm in my bunk and one of the men is verbally picking on me. I'm probably known as a wimp. But I crack, and I storm out of the bunk and pound on him. He's too startled to react, and from then on I don't get picked on.

We learn that gambling and I don't mix. There is always a crap game in the barracks. I watch, and remark on what the next roll will show. I'm right too often, and the devotees banish me because I'm a hex. Maybe they're afraid I'll want to bet.

We learn to keep in touch with the home front. We write home. After the war I will find that my letters have been saved. So have the souvenirs, like the grenade fragments from our grenade-throwing practice, and a whole bunch of later souvenirs from Europe.

We learn how to build bridges. The H-10 timber bridge, similar to the wooden trestles that railway bridges are built on, is one of our accomplishments. But the prefabricated floating bridge is our forte. Quickly setting up a bridge across an impeding river is what the Army created Light Ponton Engineers for.

The ponton bridge floats on pontons. The weight is carried on a set of open, scow-like boats made of aluminum and measuring some 18 feet long, three feet deep, and about six feet wide. These pontons are set sideways, in line with the current of a river. Over them are tied the balk, long stringers with loops on the ends so that they can be tied to the pontons. Over them in turn are laid the decking of the bridge. The pontons are anchored in the stream and a bridge like this can carry ten ton, or more if the pontons are set closer.

Another kind of ponton is the inflatable rubber one, an elongated donut with an inflated rubber sausage filling the middle. This is what will, in later years, make the recreational float boats for tenderfeet on white water such as the Colorado River.

In our knot-tying and cordage classes I show talent for learning the more complex knots. Not everyone can tie a proper double Carrick bend, for example. So my specialist number is changed. I am now a Rigger, a designation I will carry for the rest of my Army career. The irony is that I will never actually do rigging in Europe.

Our Light Equipage Platoon is in charge of two other kinds of river-crossing equipment: the footbridge and the assault boat. The footbridge is a set of rectangular boxes about a foot square in cross section and containing kapok or other flotation material so they'll still float with bullet punctures, and about eight feet long. Over these floats, tied to a line stretched across a smaller stream, are set deck sections with rope handrails. This footbridge can be quickly set up and pushed across the stream and Infantry can then run across (unfortunately, often under fire).

The assault boats are made of plywood and look like deep John boats with square sterns. These sterns can be pinned together to make a double-length, double-ended ponton. But their main use is to ferry troops across a stream by paddle. They have handrails along each side for many men to carry them at a run to the water and launch them. Several of our trucks have their racks filled with stacks of assault boats.

As a sort of finale of our Basic Training, we truck ourselves and all our equipment to Lake Murray, some 26 miles north in Oklahoma. We dig foxholes in clay that is so dry and hard that it will take a polish. In fact, I carve an imitation pipestone pipe that I still have. Then we build a bridge across a bay of the lake.

The bridge sets a record that will never be broken. Three hundred and forty-eight feet of floating bridge with ten ton capacity is constructed from scratch in two and a half hours. Air Corps flyovers and firecrackers simulate combat conditions, and we in the foxholes who are not actively taking our turn on the bridge pretend to shoot down the planes.

As a reward we are allowed to march the 26 miles back to Camp Howze with full packs. The near-dry Red River (the border between Texas and Oklahoma) never looked so good. Only a couple of more miles to "home."

Fifty years later, the events of the 13 weeks that make up Basic Training will be found indelible in memory.

Maneuvers

Basic training is over. We mark time in the queue for maneuvers, and we get to take short furloughs home. There, we're the standard heroes. This late in the war (it's a year and a half after Pearl Harbor) the civilians are pretty used to young men in uniform and we don't make as much of a stir as we would like. Our families are thrilled, though.

I buy Mom a pin at the PX. It's a small silver "castle," the symbol of Engineers, attached by a silver chain to a small heart with a blue star on a white enameled field with a red enameled border. This pin will survive the war and join my medals in their frame.

(Mothers of servicemen are authorized to put a blue star service flag in their windows. A gold star denotes that the serviceman has died in action. In the 537th, we have a song to the tune of the Georgia Tech song:
> "Mother, take down your service flag,
> Your son is an Engineer...")

We finally load up in late November and head for maneuvers. We convoy out of Camp Howze, on the northern border of Texas, and aim for the lower Texas-Louisiana border.

Our pontons at this point are the big square aluminum flat-bottom boats. Two, stacked upside down, make a semi truckload. The trip is going to take a while and our first overnight stop is at Tyler, Texas. Ever resourceful, I find that I can make a neatly covered bed between the pontons, crawling up over the bow of the bottom one. As a matter of fact this turns out to be a convenient place to stow my duffel bag, too, and even to ride part of the way in peace.

We hit our destination late in the day on Thanksgiving. Before we turn in we have to build a floating bridge across a good-sized tributary of the Sabine River. Because I'm the rigger my job is to get waist deep into the cold water and tie the parts of the bridge abutment together. The air is not much warmer and after a while it seems more comfortable to stay in the water than to get out and freeze while my drenched clothes freeze-dry. Welcome to maneuvers.

The purpose of maneuvers is to further harden us and to shake down our readiness under conditions closely approximating what we will find in a combat theater. Another purpose, and one that is wonderfully successful, is to make us glad to get out of them and into combat; we figure that it can't be any worse. We are going to come out lean and mean and ready to face anything.

We are sent for maneuvers to the Texas-Louisiana border because that's where we'll find the Sabine River. That river is tougher than any we will encounter in Europe. It's 250 feet wide and has a seven-mile current. That's a fast stream. If we can build bridges to float in that current we can make bridges anywhere. Also, we are getting into winter. That will keep down the mosquitoes and inactivate the alligators (they go torpid in the cold, as do the water moccasins), but it will prepare us to live in tents on whatever ground is available and to find out how to attain some degree of comfort.

(Bill Mauldin, the famous war cartoonist, will draw a cartoon that, while based in Italy, will depict Louisiana perfectly. Willie, sitting in the rain with his shelter half draped over his helmet, says to the young rookie sitting beside him, "A experienced field sojer will always find a way to sleep warm and dry. Lemme know when you do.")

We will bivouac near this first tributary stream of the Sabine for some time. The area isn't fully desolate, since there are some farms nearby and there is a town of sorts (Pineville) a few miles away. I work on my first mustache. One day when I'm standing guard at the entrance to our bivouac, a little girl walks by and says, "You've been drinking milk, haven't you?" so I shave.

A bivouac needs to be described, because this is the way we'll live in France most of the time, too.

Each man is issued two blankets and a shelter half. This shelter half is one half of a pup tent, a rectangle of canvas about six feet long and a bit over three feet wide, extended on one end by a triangle about three feet on a side. A set of snap fasteners is set along one edge and loops for tent pegs on the other. Two men snap their halves together, set up the folding tent poles or tie off to handy trees, and they have their sleeping quarters. The pack, helmet, duffel bag, and above all the rifle go into the tent with you to stay dry. This is home. If you set up on properly graded ground and dig drainage around the tent you sleep dry. Bad drainage, and you sleep very wet indeed, and you learn.

We get a new weapon, the bazooka. This is a shoulder-fired anti-tank rocket, a tube five feet long and four inches in diameter. It's the guide for the rocket itself. Two men fire it. One man holds the tube and lines up the sights on the target. The second man arms the rocket and slips it into the rear of the tube. When the trigger is pulled, the rocket blasts out and, since the tube is only a guide, there is no recoil.

There is something else, though, at least on the M1a1 version that we are issued. The rocket isn't finished with its blast when it leaves the muzzle and the wire screen guard at the front of the tube isn't enough. Luckily, I have stowed tweezers in the little first aid pouch on my belt. I pick bits of green plastic from the rocket, probably part of the igniter mechanism, out of the ears of the first men to fire the bazooka. This is not a weapon to fire when you're not wearing glasses.

The bazooka isn't terribly accurate but you can hit the broad side of a tank at 30 yards if you're lucky and that's all that's necessary. At its low speed the projectile wouldn't penetrate a strong cardboard box, but it isn't supposed to penetrate. In its head is a Monroe charge, a shaped charge of TNT that explodes outside the tank.

A Monroe charge has a conical cavity on its face and this focuses the blast into a forward-facing rod of force. It liquefies the steel shell of the rocket and shoots it right through tank armor. It liquefies the steel in the armor, too, and leaves a hole that looks like an oxy-acetylene cutting torch had cut it. Inside the tank that liquid steel is sprayed right through anyone in its way.

Later, we have a demonstration. We have an old junk tank set up and a razorback pig (the woods are full of them, for free) is put in the gunner's turret. Most of the bazookas miss, but the one that hits the turret paints the pig onto the far wall. Weapons of war are not supposed to be gentle, folks.

Now we settle in for maneuvers. Mostly, we build floating bridges across that @!##%@&**# Sabine River. We are given all sorts of places to build them, with most of them chosen for the difficulty of setting the abutments. Early in the game I learn how not to do it.

We are, for a change, on a location that has decent approaches to the bridge site. We are going to set up a ferry. The General in charge of the First Army then, of which we are a part, comes to watch.

The first step is to stretch a ¾ inch steel cable across the river to hold the bridge from upstream. A cable is carried across and anchored to a sturdy tree. On the near side another sturdy tree will hold the tensioning tackle. I stand beside it with a come-along, a device that will clamp onto the cable, ready to fasten the cable when it comes out of the water. The free end of the cable is pulled by our bulldozer.

I stand upstream of the cable. This is colossally dumb, but neither I nor anyone else notice that. The cable tightens, a long loop drawing up through the water where it has sagged downstream. Then the cable breaks free of the water. Two hundred and fifty feet of cable snap out of that seven mile current like a bowstring, and I'm upstream. It takes me on the point of my chin, on the helmet strap, in that narrow zone between my teeth and my Adam's apple, and I describe a graceful arc through the air. Dazed, I get up off my back, still intent on catching that cable, and I do catch it but not with the come-along. The second snap gets me right on my juvenile mustache, a chop that's fatal in judo, and I go down again. When I look up, there is Gen. Hodges hovering over me and wondering if I'm hurt. I assure him that you can't hurt a Swede by hitting him on the head, or something equally stupid. Then I get set off to the side to count stars while someone else takes the come-along to the downstream side of the cable where it belongs.

Another cable, this time in a very awkward site, nearly costs us several men. We are starting to lay out a ferry, a floating platform on two or more pontons that can be pulled from one side of the river to the other along an upstream cable. This cable has to have anchors along the way, because 250 feet is too long to avoid bowing. So several men get into an assault boat to lay the anchors. They're in full field equipment and because it's cold (late December) they're wearing their wool overcoats. And they're upstream of the cable and swept downstream.

The cable rolls the assault boat over, and suddenly we have a half dozen men in the water, weighted down and being carried away. Several of us run to grab one of the big aluminum pontons, one that takes ten paddlers, and run it down to the shore and shove off. We get all the men but a lot of equipment is lost. Natvig loses his helmet and his rifle. Dry, Natvig weighs about 140 pounds; wet, he weighs at least 250, and two of us can barely drag him into the ponton. Fortunately the men weren't in the water long enough for their overcoats to get fully soaked, and this seems to have buoyed them up long enough for us to get to them. The assault boat is a lost cause.

The bivouac here is memorable. Three events stand out: our senior officer's promotion, the great ice storm, and the loaded can of beans.

Up to now our Company Commander Maraska has been a First Lieutenant. Then his promotion comes through and he becomes Captain Maraska wearing two silver bars, the rank he'll hold for the rest of our service. He and the other officers hole up in his command tent to celebrate into the wee hours. Someone overhears, "Don't think that these railroad tracks (the dual bars) will change me. I'll be the same SOB. that I always was." True prophesy.

Everyone knows that it never gets cold in Louisiana, 'way down on the southern border of the United States. Don't believe it. The day before Christmas the rain turns into ice. We are bivouacked among what passes for hills in Louisiana, the hills rising maybe ten feet. We are in a longleaf pine forest. The trees are well spaced and the undergrowth is tolerably sparse. We are all based in pup tents and we're out working on a bridge site when the ice storm hits. We get back and find that the inch of ice that has formed on every pine needle and twig has been stripping the branches off the trees. Several tents are crushed. We allow that it's better to have to salvage tents than it would have been if we had been in them. Fortunately, the mess tent escapes. And it never gets cold in Louisiana. Hah*!*

Not all our meals are cooked. We sometimes eat C rations and sometimes K rations. The C rations (see the chapter on France) include a can of meat and beans. We have learned how to heat our rations easily: you take a five-gallon can, pour in a cupful of gasoline, light it, and drop in the cans of food and a match. You watch it carefully, and when the ends of the cans bulge you pull them out. As a machine gunner, I'm issued a big asbestos glove to handle hot gun barrels, and that's ideal for fishing out hot cans of food. Then you wait for the ends of the can to flatten again, when it's safe to open the can. Everyone carries on his dog tag chain a little hooked can opener.

My tent mate gets too impatient. He hooks the tip of the can opener on the rim of a too-hot can of beans, and punctures the can. The pressure inside has been just waiting for this. The entire contents of the can escape, homogenized, through the pinhole. And paint the inside of our tent.

We learn the uses of morphine. One of our men falls under a moving truck and breaks a leg. We reach into the little first aid pouch on his belt and get the morphine syringe. This is a needle on a tube like a miniature toothpaste tube, and we inject him. The morphine works in minutes.

Meanwhile we grind along at the practice of building bridges and ferries, and deploying assault boats and footbridges.

The semi-wild or feral hogs are a hazard while we're away from out tents. More than one of us has the experience of coming "home" at the end of the day and finding that a hog has gone in at the open end of the pup tent and rooted his way out the other end. The mess is awful. We plot revenge, if not deterrence. We conceal razor blades in oranges but never find out whether the trick works.

Louisiana is wet country. We hear that cemeteries have vaults above ground because the caskets float up out of the boggy soil otherwise. This is probably true. We dig practice foxholes in a gentle hillside (the same one where we demonstrate the bazooka) complete with fire step inside. This requires a hole over five feet deep, and it's a constant battle with the water seepage. When we come back the next day the foxholes are full of water and water is trickling out the downhill side. This water table is less than two inches below the surface, and on a hillside!

A few of the men get into the metropolis of Lake Charles, LA and we hear how rip-roaring the city is. No doubt some influence is due to the two Army bases nearby, Camp Polk and Camp Clayborne. There is a railroad running between the camps, the Clayborne and Polk or C & P, also known as Crime and Punishment. It's an Army railroad, used to train Army transportation people. It is known as the only railway in the world with a right-angle bend. Its rationale for existence here in this swamp country is that anyone who can run the C & P will be able to run any railroad. Operators have been known to look back from the caboose, and see only water; the weight of the train has pressed the roadbed into the swamp. While it was being built any equipment that slipped off the front end of the right-of-way was irretrievable. Even a locomotive is still down there somewhere. Great country for Army maneuvers.

While we are slogging away at the grunt work of maneuvers, the Big Boys are moving us pawns in war games. Sometimes we're aware of which "side" we are on, but usually we aren't. Such concerns are for the officers.

Our mood regarding the men who control our lives, the non-commissioned officers like Sergeants especially, emerges in a couple of urban legends. I guess that they express some sort of wish fulfillment. One legend is to the effect that a mean Sergeant in some other company (a location that can't be checked, of course) is found one morning standing against a tree and pinned there with a bayonet. Another legend is that a truck "accidentally" ran over a tent where a coincidentally mean Sergeant was sleeping.

We are attending to the business of getting tough and skilled and psychologically ready for assignment to a theater of war. And it works. When we complete maneuvers, we want to go and get 'em.

Oklahoma Interlude

Maneuvers are over. We are now trained soldiers, ready to go to war. But the Army doesn't want to ship us out just yet so we have to be stored somewhere. The Army, in its wisdom, chooses to store us at a camp at Ardmore, Oklahoma.

This is cold storage or relative inactivation, because we are just waiting for shipment out to the war. And it's cold, because this is winter.

The interlude is uneventful. The highlights are furloughs and a change of weapons.

Furloughs are a little more solemn now, because we won't be home after this until the war is over. I get back to Red Wing and Dad gives me a knife he made. It's impressive. The blade is a full ten inches long, made of an industrial hacksaw blade and able to whittle steel. The handle is cast of aluminum. He's made it at the motor works (marine motors) where he works as a heat treater, and it's his contribution to the war. It's also oversize for practical purposes—the trench knife that the Army issues, with a six inch blade, is more practical and portable—but I'm proud of it and am glad to take it along to Europe.

We aren't certain of our destination, but all signs point to Europe instead of the Pacific Theater. Our bridge building skills will be needed there.

The old Thompson submachine gun, which I never got to carry around anyway, doesn't reappear. Instead we will get grease guns.

Grease guns are inspired by the British Sten gun, they indeed look like a mechanic's grease gun, and they do the same thing as the Thompson but are uglier than Uzis and less accurate. The grease gun shoots the same .45 ammunition as the Thompson at about the same rate of speed. But whereas the Thompson is finely machined throughout and costs $125 -- a princely sum in the 1940s -- the grease gun has only the inside of the barrel, the face of the bolt and a couple of other parts machined. The rest are stampings. A grease gun costs $11. The bolt is a slug of steel sliding on two rods, a simple blow-back action, and the firing pin is just a projection on the face of the bolt. This means that, when the bolt slams forward, it picks up a shell and fires; all the trigger does is hold the bolt back.

The safety latch of the grease gun is the hinged cover of the shell exit port, with a lug to block the bolt. So if you pull back the bolt and close the cover as a safety catch, and then accidentally pull the trigger, the bolt may creep forward and be held only by that safety lug. If you then open the cover the bolt slams forward on a shell and... One of our men does just that while riding in a truck, and the bullet passes under the driver's knees and pulls the pin mostly out of a grenade in its box. Oh, we learn safety the hard way at times.

Anyhow, when the new grease guns come in, I get to help clean them out of the sticky Cosmolene grease and figure out how to put them together. I miss the old Thompsons. However, that's nostalgia. The grease gun weighs about half as much as the Tommy. Besides, now that I'm a Rigger, I wouldn't get the Tommy anyway.

Now after we have drilled all this time with the big Enfield and Springfield rifles we finally get our real weapons, carbines. These are little five-pound semi-automatic rifles, firing a special .30 caliber cartridge. They are much easier for an Engineer to carry about and to even wear on a sling while working, though they are not serious enough to replace an Infantryman's M-1 rifle. On the rifle range the best I can shoot with the carbine is "Qualified," (this is just above Unqualified) and I get to add a bar to my badge: "Marksman." But my carbine is beautiful, with a tiger-grain walnut stock.

There's a story to why the stock is of such high quality. The carbine was designed by a man who was in prison at the time for some offense I've forgotten. It was an elegant design that he made, a "short action, gas operated" design. When it's fired, the bolt is locked in place until the bullet has left the muzzle. A hole in the barrel a couple of inches ahead of the chamber leads down to a little cylinder. After the bullet passes the hole, a jet of explosion gas kicks back in the cylinder and rotates the bolt just enough to free it from its locked position. The bolt slams back (the bullet is gone now) and ejects the shell. As it slams forward, it picks up the next cartridge and waits for you to pull the trigger.

1970s: I buy a deer rifle from a friend. It's a Ruger .44 magnum, semi-automatic. It's a heavier version of the WWII carbine and looks just like it, only it's more accurate. With its first and only hunting shot, I take down a running deer at 100 yards. The difference is the sights, I think. The wood in the stock is ordinary straight grain walnut.

About those walnut stocks: after the carbine was designed, it was found that it could be fitted into the beautiful walnut gunstock blanks that were in storage since Germany handed them over as part of the WWI war reparations. Meanwhile, Germany went into WWII with plywood gunstocks, stronger and more practical if heavier and less beautiful.

We busy ourselves with Army routine. There is no idle time in the Army. If there is nothing else to do you march.

Then, along about May, we ship out.

I don't expect to come back. In a war you get killed. The way things are going in Europe, we are in for a grim time. We know how to kill the other guy and he knows how to kill us. I may be alone in this expectation of getting killed, but I don't think so. We have a song, a parody of the WWI song "Over There." It ends with, "We'll be over, We're going over, And we're all coming back in wooden underwear." Wooden underwear is a pine box.

The expectation of getting killed is not depressing. I have not been raised to fear dying, for one thing. And when you're young there is a certain romanticism about dying in battle. More than that, though, is what the acceptance of dying soon will do to your outlook. The proportion of things is settled by it. You don't sweat the little things as much. Fear is greatly reduced. If you're "already dead," the when and how of getting killed is less of a worry. All the rest of your life you're liberated in a way that cannot be easily expressed.

I don't quite know how this works for those who don't have a strong Christian faith. It isn't anything that is talked about, but as you prepare to fight a war you have to come to some terms with the possibility of dying. World War II is a "clean" war; we have no doubts about the necessity of doing what we are about to do and later experiences will verify that. In such circumstances you don't really have a fear of dying --just a readiness.

Prepared for discomfort (we've survived maneuvers), prepared with skill (we're the best bridge builders it the world), and prepared for any eventuality, now we can ship out when the Army needs us.

To Europe on the Liz

The time comes to leave the States for the ETO, the European Theater of Operations. All our personal gear—and all our Army issue gear—goes into the duffel bags and knapsacks or onto our belts.

We move by train and we move by stages. We cut east from Oklahoma and cross the Mississippi. A troop train isn't made for sightseeing but we do get to see that the river here is a whale of a lot wider than it is in Minnesota. No one gives us maps, no one tells us our exact route, and few of us know or care about geography enough to say just where; probably Memphis. We roll on and end up in the sugar pine sandlands of the Piedmont, in one of the Carolinas I think. We bivouac the only a night or two. The only memorable thing here is the profusion of little sundew plants, the insect eaters with sticky leaves. I've never seen a sundew before, and they're fascinating.

Then north to Camp Kilmer, New Jersey. The camp is named after the author of "Trees," I guess. We get a steak dinner upon arrival and settle very briefly into barracks life in this high-turnover camp. Camp Kilmer is a staging area for the New York harbor and units are assembled here to be loaded onto ships.

Camp Kilmer has a lot of mosquitoes and a feeling of temporariness. One memory will linger, an auditory capsule. It is bedtime, and "lights out." The PA system plays *Tatoo*, a bugle call we haven't heard before. You'd have to hear it to appreciate how it sounds and what it means.

1994 Company reunion: Crabtree, our bugler, says that he did so play Tatoo for us, but my memory doesn't agree with him.

Then by truck to New York, a short trip, and onto the loading pier. Surprise! we are going to ship out on the Queen Elizabeth.

The Liz is the world's largest ship. Built as a luxury liner, just enough bigger than the Queen Mary to take over the title, the Liz has been fitted out as a troopship. It has been stripped of most of its fancy work but the boat deck where I will live still has that mahogany rail, now entirely covered by carved initials. The corridors are paneled with matched hardwood, royal oak on our deck, and the panels have not been marred with initials. We are herded across a covered gangplank, joining 15,000 other men -- that's *fifteen thousand* on one boat -- plus a small contingent of WACs (Women's Army Corps) whom we will never see and whom we are not supposed to know about.

The Liz is going to run for it alone. German submarines are active in the Atlantic and everything else goes in convoys, escorted by destroyers. Even so the ship losses are greater than officials will admit. If the Liz were to go in a convoy it would have to chug along at convoy speed, and it would be the biggest, easiest, and most attractive target there. So it's less risky for the Liz to go alone. With its nearly 30 knots' speed it can outrun a submarine and it cuts an irregular course across the ocean. I have just turned 20.

We leave at an unannounced time, just taking off with not so much as a whistle. Meanwhile we have been bunked in and jammed into our limited space.

One man to a bunk. The bunk is a pipe frame with a canvas sling stretched over it. Onto its 2X6 foot space goes the man and everything he "owns." There is no room on the floor except a narrow corridor when the bunks are let down for the night. The bunks are stacked five high and end to end. I draw the second bunk from the bottom.

Although the Liz is big it's not completely immune to the motion of the ocean. There are no motion sickness pills in 1944 and not everyone is a born sailor. I experiment. If I loop my canvas web belt over the frame of the bunk above I can sleep with my head literally in a sling, minimizing the ship's roll. Besides, we don't have pillows. Unlike a few others I do not have to go to the rail and sacrifice to Neptune.

The trip will take three and a half days. With this huge contingent of men, rigid time schedules are necessary for feeding. Some group is always at the mess. The cooks are, on this Cunard liner, British. "British cook" is an oxymoron. Coffee is made in stainless steel vats six feet high and stirred with a military (olive drab painted) canoe paddle. We aren't going to starve to death in three days so many of the men are not hungry at chow time.

Half way out there is a sudden racket. The gunners on the top deck are "holding practice." The main weapon is a bank of rocket tubes, and they fire salvos at imaginary targets a mile out. The impact zone is churned to froth. The idea is that any submarine lying in wait for the Liz would have to be on the surface to keep up, and those rockets would blow up the sub before it could get close enough to fire a torpedo. Maybe, for all we know, the target isn't imaginary. At any rate, neither on this trip nor on the many others taken by the Liz does a sub get close.

> *After the war, Cornell sends me a book written about the Liz. Great pictures, including of the bunks, and statistics on the number of men on each voyage.*

Latrines are flushed with salt water and the water in the taps is salt also. Only drinking water is fresh. This poses a problem for grooming because soap will not lather in salt water. So we are introduced to a great new invention: non-soap detergent. It's a small yellowish bar that acts like soap otherwise, but that will give a sort of lather in the salt water. Little do we know it, but this is the dawn of a new era in detergents and that little bar will replace almost all soaps in the next few years. At the moment it's just a novelty that only some of us notice.

The ship plows on and early on the fourth day out we see a misty green line of land off the starboard. It grows a bit and gains a lumpy profile. This is Ireland, and we are now steaming north to our as yet unannounced destination.

Open water, and then through the opening in the submarine nets across the mouth of the Firth of Clyde. We are going to dock at Glasgow.

Well, not "dock." We drop anchor out in the Firth. We will go ashore next morning in lighters.

Now the rumors firm up into real news, brought by the lighter crews. This morning Europe was invaded. This is D-Day! We don't know any details, but this is indeed the big day.

In New York men could file onto the Liz from several gangplanks and fill it fairly quickly. Here, transferred by boat to the shore, we take a longer time. The Liz opens a huge side door to give access to the lighters.

We do not move in a complete unit of 200 men here and somehow the Company has to re-assemble somewhere. We won't get together as a unit in Glasgow. Some men are detailed to stay and pick up equipment. The rest of us go onto trains for the ride south to our destination in England.

One memorable observation in Glasgow before our train pulls out. I notice a lot of children about, and assume that they're evacuees from London and the south of England, where cities are bombed a lot. I ask a Scotsman beside the track if this isn't who the kids are. He says, "Na'. They'rrre al' ourrrs. We do verrry weel forrr ourrrsel's."

England

The train ride south into England is lost on me except for some random flashes of rolling hills seen in the twilight. We travel mostly at night, blacked out, through a black countryside. We emerge at Uttoxeter in Staffordshire in the midlands.

We are billeted at Crakemarsh Hall, one of the manor homes of Lady Astor. It is a castle-y pile, stone and pinnacles. The roof is covered in sheet lead and there is a parapet around the base of the roof. I've never seen a lead roof before, and I enjoy strolling around behind the parapet. For quarters, we sort ourselves into the various rooms and floors.

In front of the manor home are acres of formal approach, with the road winding through holly trees. One day as I walk some distance from the manor home, a plane glides over. It is like a DC-3 in general conformation, but slimmer. It has two engine nacelles under its wings, and they are long and slim. No propellers! It's one of those jets we have read about. Actually, it's a Glouchester Meteor, the first Allied jet, but that information is classified and unavailable to us. But I recognize it as a jet on the basis of "forecast" stories in *Popular Science* of the 1930s.

We aren't good houseguests. One day, I'm about to open the big oak door to my room, when with a bang about six inches of blade grows out of the door. Dagger Wallace is practicing his bayonet throwing. If I'd opened that door a couple of seconds sooner, I would have been perforated.

> *Even so, Crakemarsh Hall will survive many years more. When Ruth and I visit Uttoxeter in the early 2000s and want to see it, we're told that it was demolished a couple of years earlier.*

Our motor pool is at Locksley Hall, closer to Uttoxeter. We spend a lot of time at Locksley Hall because all our equipment is being readied there.

Back in the woods from Locksley is a queer stone structure, known locally as "Friar Tuck's Chapel." It isn't any such thing, of course. It's part of the facade of the manor home that was burned down in the 1700s. It's set in a neat little, narrow forest of yew trees, and I take a twig as a souvenir of the tree that may be descended from the tree that Robin Hood made his bow from.

You see, this Locksley Hall is the home of Robin Hood. It may be only part of the manorial estate, because the ruins of a Norman-type castle down the road is no doubt where he was established in his fief by King Richard. Alas for the Robin Hood of Ivanhoe and other romances; King Richard was succeeded by Prince John, who would not have left Robin Hood's head on his shoulders. We will never know exactly what happened to Robin, the product of a marriage between a Norman and a Saxon. In any event he's dead now. But, insofar as the legends are true, and there seems to be some truth to them, this is his family estate.

Back among the yew trees I practice-fire my little .25 caliber automatic pistol. I carry it as my personal side arm in Europe, though it is too weak to be a serious weapon. Fortunately I will never have to use it.

On one side of the yard area is a "ha-ha." This is a peculiarly English device, designed to enclose the deer park. The yard ends in a vertical drop-off of maybe six feet, then a moat that slopes up onto the field. When you approach a ha-ha from the manor house side, you don't see anything. The ground seems to continue level. To the deer on the other side, the slope gives no purchase for jumping the moat, and the wall seems to be higher than it is. Now, of course, there are no deer in the park, which has been converted to farmland pasture.

The manor home is fairly elegant. Inside there is a sweeping stair with curved oak banister. And a library, which has been treated unkindly by previous users. Books are scattered on the floor. I rescue a leather-bound volume, "The Elements of Heraldry," printed in

1777. In later years I will find that this is a rare and valuable book. It contains text explaining all the heraldic conventions and terms, and pictures of dozens of coats of arms. Many of the pictures are hand colored. The last page of the book looks like a mistake that should have been removed before binding. It's a note that says, "The Printer is Instructed to Beat the Book before any of the Plates are Placed Therein," because with the printing technology of the time, ink would transfer from the printed pages to the pictures. Books were literally beaten to make them flat after printing.

> *I eventually sent the book home. Then I lent it, and it didn't come back and the lender put me off -- I think she either accidentally damaged it or lent it to someone else. In later years, when I returned to Locksley Hall and found it to be a school for neurologically impaired children, I wanted to return the book but couldn't. The book has been reproduced in CD and I did send a copy of that to the school, with no response.)*

In the yard is a dovecote. It looks like a stubby silo with holes around it. In earlier years people kept doves to supply meat and eggs. Inside the cote are stairs and balconies that allow the backs of the pigeon nest boxes to be opened to remove the eggs and squabs.

On evening passes, we truck into the cities of Stafford and Derby. It takes most of the month we are there to learn how to understand the Midlands accent of the local people. In spite of the common English saying that the matter with American soldiers is that we're "overfed, overpaid, oversexed, and over here," the locals are as friendly as one could ask. We learn to appreciate warm Coke and meat pies and jam tarts. Everyone is pleased that the Allies are finally getting on with the business of invading the continent.

> *On return visits in the 1970s and 1990s I find that the language isn't so strange. Maybe my ear has been converted, or else the language of England*

has been homogenized in the intervening years. Mass media do tend to homogenize a country's language.

In the early 2000s Ruth and I go back to Uttoxeter. We had contacted some local sources on the Internet to get information, and the local newspaper wanted an interview. The writeup is pretty accurate, and it implies that we are the only ones who have checked back. The Internet also informs us that Uttoxeter has an interesting history and quite a bit of WWII history of events that we didn't know about then.

As the invasion proceeds, room is made for us in southern England. We truck down to the Salisbury Plains and tent out on the downs for another month.

Now we use our pup tents. The weather is fine most of the time and camping out isn't at all bad. There is plenty for us to do with our equipment, getting it fully ready for the crossing and for action on the continent.

Passes now are to Salisbury, ten miles away. Another local resident accent to get used to, but an easier one this time. I get to see the famous Salisbury cathedral, with its bending column and its clock mechanism, and with its steeple reaching 501 feet into the air.

I also get to see something I've wanted to see for years, Stonehenge. No one else in the company seems to have ever heard of it, and no one else is interested in an expedition to go see it. So one day I ask a Bobby, a policeman on the Salisbury street, how to get there. On his advice I rent a taxi and am driven out to Stonehenge. We pass the mound of Old Sarum and drive out onto the plains.

I didn't go up to Old Sarum then, and had only a sketchy idea of what it is. In later years I've been to that site twice. It's unique, a former Iron Age Celtic hill fort, then a Roman fort, then a Norman

*stronghold.   Now it's a ruin that gives a great
overview of the Salisbury plain.*

There Stonehenge stands.   There is no one about.   It's
as solitary as if the makers had just walked off and left it.
I walk all over area, pat the great standing stones, lean
on the "blood stone."   I pace off the line to the Heel
Stone, and sight along it to the low barrows and avenues
left by the Old Ones.   I the distance rises the conical hill
of Silbury.

The ring of Aubrey holes around Stonehenge has been
cleared down to the chalk but not all of them can be
identified.   I walk under the lintels, marveling at the
people who raised the huge blocks of stone in an age
when there were no engines.   Like everyone else until
decades later, I miss seeing the "maker's trademarks,"
the Mycenaean dagger and double axe engraved on one
of the uprights that mark the monument as the probable
work of a Minoan contractor.

*When my first wife Bernice and I come back to
England in 1983 or so and visit Stonehenge, the
fence is up and there are guards and admission
prices.   And you're not allowed to actually walk
among the stones any more.   Progress.*

*We also get to walk around in the town of Avebury
and visit its little museum, and see Silbury Hill --
which has yielded nothing to archaeologists.   The
countryside seems to be somehow more densely
occupied than it did in 1944.*

On all the stones of Stonehenge in 1944 I can find only
one set of scratched initials.   Vandalism is not yet in
style.   The taxi driver, who has seen this before, waits in
the cab and then drives me back to Salisbury.

Little happens while we are on the Salisbury Plains,
except that one of the .50 caliber machine guns nearly
takes off my finger.   Stripping it on a post mount, I am
down to the 54-pound receiver and have pulled its
forward mounting pin, then pulled the mount's elevation

45

lock pin. The receiver swings up and back, pivoting on its back pin, and clips part way through a finger caught between it and the post mount. The medics decide that it doesn't need stitches, and tape it shut.

> *The scar is still there, middle finger left hand, and feeling returned to the finger tip in somewhat over a year.*

Once, not more than a half mile away, a German V-1 or buzz bomb putts past. I can see it clearly. These unmanned cigars with the stubby wings are essentially unguided missiles. They can maintain a steady low altitude and run until they are out of fuel. Then the shutter-jet dies, and the flying bomb falls and explodes. They are designed to be instruments of terror, and Hitler expects the English to be so demoralized that they will give up. He had said that he'd wring the neck of the English like a chicken; Churchill said, "Some chicken! Some neck!"

Another day is more demoralizing to me. A small flight of Hurricane Hawkers, the British fighters with the offset radiators, roars over at treetop level, going somewhere urgently. Accustomed to the quiet of the plains, I want to roll up in a ball because of the sudden and pounding racket. The planes are over and gone in seconds.

The time comes to cross the Channel and take up positions in France. We have been in England for nearly two months.

> *It would be nice to find that bivouac site again. I've been back to that area twice and none of the countryside looks familiar. I guess that even England changes over time.*

Across France: the Great Rat Race

We have spent our time on the Salisbury plains keeping our equipment in shape and waiting. No one knows when we will move out. As bridge builders, we vaguely know that we won't be needed until the front begins to move and there are rivers to cross.

April, 1944: I was in London. The timing was right for a trip to France, where I had not been since fifty years previously. I persuaded Daughter Katy (Kathleen) to meet me in London and to travel the French route with me.

I am sort of in charge of the company's 14 .50 caliber machine guns. They're set in ring mounts above the cabs of the trucks and we've been having trouble with the cartridge belts. Every time the truck is driven and the mount is vibrated, cartridges tend to work loose from the fabric belts. The belts edge to the front of the ammunition boxes and the cartridges edge out of their belts, and the gun becomes useless. We jam the cartridges back into the belts, and they work loose again. The guns would be able to get off maybe two shots each and then stop.

We've heard that metal link belts are coming, and they won't have that problem. Technology will catch up with us later.

The word comes that we're moving out. We break camp and load everything into our 75 vehicles: four jeeps, the Diamond-T wrecker, the bulldozer, the air compressor, and lots of trucks. My gun is mounted on the air compressor truck, with three of us assigned to what will become our home for the next month: Ron Cornell, the compressor operator; Evert Cox, the driver; and me. Cornell is an older man, maybe as old as thirty. Cox drives just fine in spite of the fact that he has one eye angled outward. We joke that he can scan both ditches at the same time.

It is dark when we leave. Each driver follows the double cat's-eye blackout light of the truck ahead. No other lights, of course.

In the dark our convoy moves slowly. There is nothing to see, of course. When we stop I go to check some of the machine guns. Out of 14, only two are operational. The rest are disabled by those fabric belts. Fortunately, no one is in the sky; the German planes don't come over England much any more, and when they do, they don't waste time on convoys.

It is still dark when we start the descent into the Portsmouth area. The impression will remain 50 years later of a long hill on a tree-lined road. (Since my memory is blank about loading, we must have begun to do that while it was still dark.)

> *1994: At Portsmouth, there is little to show us where to go. Katy and I go into the terminal and change our money into Francs, and find out what we can. We are in the right place.*

> *We are all ticketed and there is one tall car ferry loading cars and trucks. The ferry moves smoothly out of the harbor and we are off down the channel that passes to the east of the Isle of Wight. The port shore is marked by a string of lights for some time. No lights in 1944.*

1944: We are scattered among a number of landing craft, LSTs (Landing Ship, Tank). The ships are manned by casual but alert veterans of the channel crossing, who mind their 40 mm Bofors guns. We are crossing in daylight. However, we learn that the day before a breakthrough was made in the hedgerow county around St. Lo in Normandy, so all available German planes will be busy there instead of in the Channel.

Some of us doze to make up for lost sleep of last night.

> *1994: I had arranged to rent a car in Cherbourg. The plan was to then drive to Utah Beach, where I had landed on D-59 in 1944, and to drive the exact*

48

French route of the 537th as best we could. A bit over 2000 kilometers of nostalgia and sightseeing.

D-59, 1944, 59 days after D-Day: The LST noses onto the flats at Utah Beach and the front opens. The trucks roll out and grind up through gaps in the sand ridge that sits above high tide. More sand flats. We scatter out and settle down for the night.

A marvel appears. It is a post-hole auger mounted on the rear of a truck, the first we farm boys have seen, and it is digging holes to serve as latrines. The holes, the size of telephone poles, are faster than digging by hand and easier to fill than a slit trench.

France seems like an empty land. There are remains of defenses, but nothing else standing. Inland the terrain is low and flat, boggy in places. We have landed.

> *1994: the ferry is slipping into the Cherbourg harbor and dawn is greyly breaking. The customs man appears and signals us forward. He looks at our passports and waves us on. There were no passport controls in 1944*

The beach here is nearly flat and 200 feet wide. Then comes a ridge of sand dune, marking the limit of storm waves, about a dozen feet high and breached by roadways.

> *.1944: It is not hard to find the road we want, the one that leads out of Cherbourg to St. Mere Eglise, from where we can turn off to Utah Beach. St. Mere Eglise was the first French town liberated in 1944, by parachute troops. One of its claims to fame is that a paratrooper got hung up on the church steeple and had to dangle there all day, playing dead, until the town was taken and he could dare to move.*

> *The 101st Airborne made the assault on St. Mere Eglise for good reason. Utah Beach was less well defended than was Omaha and the others, even though its sand flats make a better landing area. Apparently the Germans counted on the marshy area*

behind the beach to be impassable, and counted on the Allies to be sensible and leave that beach alone. The airborne assault was made to secure the few passes across the marshes, and it worked. We didn't appreciate that fact in 1944. Now, in daylight, it's clear why things happened the way they did.

A loop of barbed wire concertina is eroding out of the dune, so rusted that I can easily snap off a length of it, a souvenir of Utah Beach 1944.

A memorial is being built for this year of the 50th anniversary of D Day. The concrete shell is up but the interior isn't finished. We walk past the new memorial building—the sign beside the path says "Utah Beach"—and out through the gap in the line of dunes.

There it is, flat and windswept. All the 1944 barriers are gone, and all that can be seen over the dune line is the curve of the memorial and a German artillery piece (an 88) on the skyline to the left. The beach is strewn with shells, the mollusk kind this time.

D-60, 1944: (Our departure from the beach is another blur in my memory. I think it was at night.) We make a curious loop in getting on with our move. We drive inland a ways to St. Mere Egilse, then turn north to Montebourg, Valognes, and Briquebec before turning south again. Cherbourg is still held by a large German force at the submarine pens there, though the front to our south is wildly fluid in the wake of the St. Lo breakthrough. Some of our men report being fired upon at Briquebec, our farthest north point on the peninsula. As it turns out, the German garrison at Cherbourg will be left to wither while the campaign is pursued to the south by a major part of the Third Army, the 537th included.

Whether we pause in our trek I won't recall. But it is night when we travel south along the western side of the peninsula, and a wild night it is. Near Coutances we are passing through an area where a US anti-aircraft battery is deployed when a German ME-109 strafes the road.

The convoy ahead of us and the convoy behind us get most of the fire. We have the engine of one truck shot out. But the spectacular part of the night (apart from my knowledge that our own machine guns still don't work) is the friendly fire. The anti-aircraft battery is armed with "wasp wagons," trailers that each has four .50 caliber machine guns driven by servomotors, with the gunner sitting in the middle with a single handle and trigger. The tracers arch over us like swords at a military wedding, lancing up in high parabolas. As far as I can tell the ME-109 gets away.

1994: Avranches comes in sight. It's daylight this time, and we can see that the town is built on a hill beside a stream. Just off the main street through town is the church, a building that must have been restored and that most people would call a cathedral.

We drive on through the rest of Avranches. There is the little river, with its bridge. Not a trace of wartime destruction to be seen.

1944: We of the 537th will remember Avranches quite well. Our convoy gets through the town, still a bit shaken by the strafing at Coutances. We cross a bridge over a small river. By now our company is somewhat strung out along the road, and we who are in the front part miss out on the excitement. Our rear trucks get across the bridge when German tanks rumble back to retake the town. On friendly advice, some of our men hide their vehicles behind buildings until the tanks go past, then they catch up.

Fine. Now we're cut off. We had cut across the peninsula south of the Germans at Cherbourg, now other Germans cut across behind us. Never mind. We have momentum, and we just keep going. Someone with strategic oversight has sent several units of the Third Army due south, through the confusion of the broken front, to cut off the Brest peninsula, the pointy part of France that juts into the Atlantic south of England. Our company is attached to the south-blitzing corps of

51

the Third Army (now commanded by General George Patton, who will be our commander for the rest of the war), because there will be rivers to bridge if the Germans have the organization necessary to blow the existing bridges. The Loire and Maine rivers are down there, at Angers.

The hedgerows of this part of France are a conspicuous feature in 1944. A hedgerow is a peculiarly European object. Over the centuries farmers tossed the rocks to the edge of the field, not so much to make a wall as to get rid of the rocks. Nature consolidated them. Dirt cemented them and the roots of bushes wove them into solid walls three to six feet thick and up to eight feet high. From a military standpoint this makes great defensive terrain. A rifle bullet won't go through them, but more importantly they give concealment.

This is a significant part of the reason why it took 58 days for D-day to lead to the Great Rat Race, as we call the run through France after the breakthrough at St. Lo.

The invading US troops were reduced to taking the territory field by small field because of the hedgerows. When you approach a hedgerow, you understand, the other guy is somewhere behind it while you are advancing across an open field where he can pick you off.

American ingenuity produced the hedgerow plow. Tanks were fitted with notched blades in front, and they plowed their way through the hedgerows, to be followed by infantry. The German lines gave way at St. Lo, and chaos took over. Now we are just in time to join the flood into France, the Great Rat Race.

1994: Now we are off the Cherbourg peninsula. The country opens before us, though of course from a car you can't see any difference. The roads are good, wide enough and smoothly paved with asphalt. In 1994, the sense of something missing resolves into an observation: most of the hedgerows are gone. The fields are bigger and the nature of agriculture has changed. The hedgerows mostly had to go, and they went. There are a few, and maybe there are more of them off to the left, in the true hedgerow country, but along our road it's different now.

Our second night out from the beach we nearly lose an officer at a hedgerow. We pull into some fields for the night, and guards are posted all over. We are all nervous, what with knowing that there are Germans behind us (though we don't know whether there were enough of them to worry about). The orders to the guards are to call "Halt!" three times before shooting, though; this is normal guard protocol.

The night is pretty dark, being overcast and with a new moon. In the middle of the night a Lieutenant who shall remain nameless gets conscientious about his duties as officer of the guard. He goes to each post to see if everyone is alert, and (as some of us think) he's sort of trying to sneak up on them. He comes to a gap in the hedgerow on our perimeter where Zwak has been posted. You need to remember that Zwak is one of the smaller guys, a Minnesota farm boy from north of St. Cloud, a math whiz but very quiet in speech and demeanor. Very quiet.

So the Lieutenant goes up to the post, and he can see the gap in the hedgerow in the nearly pitch dark, but he can't see Zwak. This could be serious because we are deep in what might be enemy territory. If we've lost a guard there may be more trouble.

No Zwak. Finally, the Lieutenant goes right up to the hedgerow and is about to walk through. He hears on his left the "click!" of a gun safety being eased off, and the quiet voice of Zwak saying "Halt" for the third time.

Farm boys can see in the dark. That Lieutenant will never check another guard post at night for the rest of the war.

Normandy, even in 1994, is picturesque in its own way. The farm building clusters have their individual character, being built of gray stone, low, and severely rectangular. There are normal trees because, in fifty years, trees have had time to mature again, though there aren't as many in roadside rows as I remember.

1944: We move more slowly now. The front is consolidating somewhat ahead of us and to our left, but there is still not much for bridge builders to do. We bivouac long enough to get some feel for the land. We are on the edge of the Breton country and the few people we do "talk" with have a distinct non-Parisian accent. In our youthful ignorance, we can't put our fingers on it, though I am vaguely aware of the meaning of the Brest Peninsula and that the old speech is Breton, a Celtic language.

There are trees and bushes. We usually bivouac out of the way of towns. We eat a lot of C rations.

(For the uninitiated: C rations come in six cans for the day, each can a bit bigger than the cans that cocktail wieners come in. Three cans are the main part of the meal; for each day, one can of meat and vegetable hash, one can of meat and vegetable stew, and one can of meat and beans. The contents of the first two are exactly what Hormel, the contractor, will sell to the civilian market for another 60+ years. The beans are just like Campbell's and probably are. And the other three cans each contain: four or five dog biscuits; a packet of the newly-invented, not quite perfected instant coffee, or a packet of lemonade mix, or a packet of cocoa; sugar to go with the coffee; hard candy or tropical chocolate; and three cigarettes. The dog biscuits are round, dry, solid crackers made of what is good for you: whole wheat, and probably a protein supplement. Those six cans will keep you going all day, and I don't recall being hungry.)

On the move the meat cans from the C rations can be wired to the truck's exhaust manifold, and they're hot for lunch. Being unconventional I cut a set of chopsticks from a bush to use instead of my spoon, since we don't

54

have dishwashing facilities. You can eat with those things, standing up in the gun's ring mount and jolting along the road.

On the bushes in Brittany there are snails aestivating, because it's summer. They're bigger than marbles and smaller than golf balls, and they're glued to the branches and sealed with their dried slime. We know that the French eat those things, but we sure aren't going to.

1994: On through Vitre and Laval, and then due south toward Angers. The road is unreeling steadily, and I'm not tired. Katy is planning to take some pictures of farm buildings, when we realize that we're out of Normandy, and the character of the farm buildings has changed. Too late to get pictures of the Norman farms. As I'd forgotten, each region of France has its own style of farmstead, except that all of them consist of clusters of buildings packed tightly together.

As we near Angers I mention to Katy that it was about here that we realized, back in 1944, that we were traveling without good intelligence and communication, and the Germans had less.

1944. We know that we are getting close to Angers, because there are road signs. None of us knows anything about Angers, its significance or its size. But we do notice something that is significant. We pass some infantry riflemen, and they're in the ditches. Maybe they're resting, but maybe not. They all have their rifles pointed forward, up the road. They may know something that we don't. We've gone far enough and pull off the road into hedgerowed fields.

Although there has been no enemy fire since Avranches, we still each dig a shelter trench to sleep in at night. I dig mine beside the air compressor truck, near the base of the hedgerow. A shelter trench is six feet long, about 20 inches wide, and deep enough to put me below ground level. Then I've done my work for the day.

I climb up on the hedgerow for a better view of the countryside and stand there for a few minutes. I can't see Angers, which I visualize to be another medium-sized town. All I can see ahead through the trees is a church steeple. So that's Angers? Then I notice a snapping sound in the air, and then a couple of twigs fall from the bushes beside me. Those are bullets! The bugger is trying to kill me! I jump down from that hedgerow a whole lot less casually than I climbed up.

I'm not the only one who notices the bullets, and the word is passed. Later, we learn that a tank was detailed to get rid of the sniper, and cleaned him out with one shot on the church tower. War is hard on buildings.

The day isn't done with me yet. As I start to prepare my shelter trench for sleeping I notice that a small snake has fallen in. The shape of his head says "viper," though of course I don't know European snakes. So I get a stick and pin down its neck and take it out of the trench. With a smaller stick I pry its mouth open and two fangs drop down into position. It's a viper, all right. I don't know how strong his poison is, but maybe he's what my Norwegian-born Mom called a "høgg-orm," and he definitely is poisonous. I kill the poor thing and decide to sleep on the truck's toolbox tonight. That's the first of two shelter trenches I will dig in France and not use, this one because I suddenly don't feel like it.

1994: Katy and I drive into Angers, and we discover that it's quite a big city. It's more crowded with people than we've seen in other cities like Laval. There is even a sort of superhighway that cuts alongside the downtown area, and there is a respectable-sized river beside it. This is categorically bigger than what we saw in 1944. One church steeple doesn't make a city.

Angers is old. It was the capital of Anjou, a "country" that rivaled France and Normandy a thousand years ago. Guidebooks that weren't available in 1944 (the Army used National Geographic *maps—honest!) now tell how the House of Anjou became the Angevin Kings of England, starting with Henry II. It has had plenty of time to build itself up, and it's big, about the size of St. Paul. Its streets are now a mix of open, fast-moving avenues contrasted with the twisted streets in the medieval section on the acropolis where traffic crawls.*

We head for where the train station ought to be, because that's where the hotel we tried to reserve is located. We do get into the downtown and hotel district, and even spot "our" hotel, but the traffic is hopeless. There are a lot of hotels, and no place to park. We cruise.

As we cruise, we get up on the acropolis beside the famous cathedral and castle. I get into a blind turnoff that looked like the entrance to a parking area, and have to back out into traffic and I bash the bumper into a post. Neither object is marred, and no one hits us -- or even honks, though the back of the car sticks out into traffic. In the past fifty years, the French have had a revolution in horn etiquette.

We find a small motel designed for truckers on the outskirts of Angers. Next day we are up and out at what is the normal hour for us, but that is early by European standards.

We didn't get enough of "downtown" Angers last night, so we drive back to the acropolis and park beside the cathedral. Breakfast is on the street, bought at markets and the bakery. Katy is impressed by how friendly and courteous the French are. Of course they are -- we aren't in Paris, and we greet the proprietor with a smile and "Bo' jour, M'sieur!" before looking around.

We are able to get into the cathedral. Just about no one else is around. The interior is like that of all old European cathedrals -- stony, tall, unheated -- it must be miserable in the winter. But the beauty of the place makes up for all that. The arches soar and *cross overhead, the light comes through the stained glass windows. The windows date from the 12th through the 16th centuries, the stone fabric from the 12th. We wander around at will.*

Then out and down the long flight of stairs, at least a drop of 150 feet, down to the fountain at the bottom.

In 1944, the acropolis or city height is another thing I never knew about Angers, though one of our platoons did go to the city but didn't enlighten me. The cathedral we might expect, though I naively think that the church steeple with the sniper is "the church" at Angers. But this acropolis, with its grand staircase from the fountain in the valley up to the cathedral at the top, is something we have no way to visualize. And the castle is certainly something we GIs never heard about.

The castle was built and rebuilt over the centuries. First constructed in the ninth century, it was destroyed and the present structure dates mainly from about 1238. Angers, Anjou, the adjective Angevin—all the same word, and now it comes together. The Plantagenets (beginning with Henry II, the Lion in Winter) of Anjou were also kings of England. This was the family home of Richard the Lionhearted and Prince John, and their mother, Eleanor of Aquitane.

The castle is mortised into the living rock and rises sheer to a great height all around except where it joins the acropolis. We walk along the riverward edge, and the increasingly steep rock becomes more and more castle wall as we go until only the foundation is native rock. A postern gate comes down an artificial crevice in the rock.

Then to the right-hand side, the tallest side of the castle. There are 17 round towers in the wall, many of them on this side, and the height is daunting. It would take a foolish enemy to attack from this quarter. The moat begins, a wide square ditch that cuts off the castle from the acropolis, as we climb the hill along the right side.

Then along the uphill side. The moat here is deep and square, and the bottom now is a formal garden. In pre-gunpowder days the top of the wall would be within bowshot, but by the same token an attacker on this flat acropolis would be exposed also. The final side, toward the cathedral, is less imposing and it would be the easiest approach, if any approach were easy, in spite of the moat. The defensive wall must have enclosed the whole acropolis in the old days, at least enclosing the cathedral. In time of siege the defender would have leveled the townspeople's houses up here to deprive an attacker of cover.

In WWII, the castle was bombed by Americans because it was a munitions depot. That must have been spectacular, but we sure didn't know about it. The bombing must have taken place before we got near, probably months earlier.

In 1944, we must have pulled out of Angers routinely, because I have no memory of it.

The Great Rat Race through France is on. We have not paused anywhere for very long nor will we, and Angers was the longest. Third Army logistics are, in retrospect, impressive. We have got all our supplies on time and we have enough rations and gas to move along.

What we don't have is bathing facilities. We will not have proper baths or showers for a month. We are all beginning to look and smell a bit ratty. The washbasin is the helmet shell and it's OK but too small for much beyond shaving. We are all young (I'm 20 now) and shaving isn't a big priority. I let the fuzz grow. None of the officers is much better off, so no one disciplines us for failing to show parade ground grooming.

Bill Maulden has an appropriate cartoon. Willie and Joe, disheveled as usual, are lounging on some steps under the disapproving gaze of an

59

officer, and Willie says, "He's right, Joe. When we ain't fightin we ought to look like sojers."

The roads are gravel and it hasn't rained much. This is a mixed blessing. Living outdoors as we do we appreciate dry weather. On the other hand the roads are dusty. A column of 75 vehicles, such as we have, kicks up quite a bit of dust. I'm grateful that our vehicle, the air compressor truck, is in First Platoon and consequently isn't at the tail of the convoy. We roll along through rural France, stopping every couple of hours for piss call. That is when we all line up beside the road and relieve ourselves. There are no civilians around usually, and if any French people happen by, they pay no notice; they're used to soldiers and their native urinals on the street (pissoires) are not enclosed in the back anyway.

As we roll along the roads there are occasional sections where combat engineers have cleared the roadblocks. This is where retreating troops cut down the rows of trees with explosive scissors charges to lay them across the road, interlaced like locked fingers, as a delaying tactic. Tracked vehicles like tanks of course take to the fields. Smart and organized retreating troops mine those fields. In 1944, at this stage of their retreat, the German troops are not organized.

At about this time (actually, July 20), some of Hitler's generals try to kill him with an exploding briefcase. He escapes unhurt, but his paranoia is activated. He orders that all field communications be sent to Berlin and then relayed back to the recipient. This procedure is great for hindering conspiracies, but disastrous for timely field communications.

There is one night during this run that some of us will long remember. We halt for the night and remain strung out along the road. This stringing out prevents our becoming a concentrated target but now it has another purpose. A large pocket of Germans, the Seventh Army I believe, has been pocketed between the US First Army to the north and us in the Third Army cutting northeast toward Paris. Now the pocketed German troops are cut off. They are a big bunch complete with several infantry divisions, panzer (tank) divisions, and artillery. If they were to turn south they could walk through the strung-out US Third Army as if it were paper.

We know our situation and we sweat out the night. We are 200 men with carbines and fourteen .50 caliber machine guns holding a couple of miles of road. I tour the guns again, and again most of them are inoperative. I draw guard duty and stand in the ring mount of my machine gun. It's not a good night for sleeping.

The Germans don't know the situation. Thanks to Hitler's order they can't communicate among themselves effectively. They don't have any adequate aerial reconnaissance either, so they bunch up and await capture. The night passes without incident and we go on.

> *1994: As we drive through the towns Katy and I are impressed by the silence of small-town streets. Ghost towns.*

1944. The dust of the roads drops away when we pass through the paved streets of towns and cities. In this part of France the towns were not bombed and shelled. And the people are out in force to welcome us.

The newspaper pictures of people cheering and giving flowers and wine to the GIs are correct. We have just liberated them from several years' occupation by German troops. The German presence may not have been intrusive out here, but to the French the occupation has been humiliating. They are mightily glad to see us and they want to show it.

My convoy position is in the ring mount of my machine gun. You recall that this means standing on the seat of the air compressor truck, with the floor of the cab filled with first a layer of sand bags (in case we hit a mine), and then a dozen boxes of .50 caliber shells and a half dozen boxes of hand grenades.

The air compressor truck is unlike any of the others and it must be mysterious to the onlookers. It has the nose and open-top cab of an Army truck and also its standard double-dual rear wheels. But in place of the canvas-hooded rack the back is occupied by a long engine hood with two-foot-wide tool boxes running beside it, a crosswise big tool box ahead of it, and a crosswise cylindrical air tank with hose spools in the rear. Then, more exposed than on regular trucks, there is the ring mount with a big machine gun and a dust-covered GI (me) standing inside it. I think that some of the people believe that this is the company commander. In any event, our truck gets more than its share of gifts, with Cox and Cornell grinning as broadly as I am.

Courville appears. Again, there is nothing that recalls the way it looked fifty years ago. It might as well be any small French city. There is a bridge over a modest river, maybe fifty feet across and down about ten feet from the street level. Neither it nor the area around it looks familiar.

1944. (Was it here at Courville, west of Paris, or was it south at Yonne, or was it to the east of the city, that we built that H-10 bridge? I can see it now, many years later and could draw the scene. No matter, it was somewhere similar.)

At a small French city, a stream runs just beyond the main town. I have traded a 4-ounce bar of chocolate (a D ration) for a loaf of that sour, heavy black peasant bread that I will never find again after leaving France and spend half the day relishing it. Our job here is to replace a bridge that the Germans have blown. The bridge was reinforced concrete, and it has been blown expertly. The tangle that is left will have to be jackhammered out before we can build.

The bar piers and surface slabs of the bridge are a jumble and the air compressor is chugging away and the jackhammer is adding its racket. As chunks of concrete are broken off and their reinforcing rods cut with a torch we haul them off.

Captain Maraska wears polished brown paratrooper boots, gotten from who knows where. We all think they're pretentious. He stands on the remains of the bridge, supervising. Then the slab he's standing on cracks and sags and he goes down with it, a drop of only a couple of feet. But he's trapped. The crack has gripped the heel of his boot and it tries to squeeze him out of it like toothpaste. He yells and it appears that he'll need to get to a medic. I run to his jeep (officially, I'm assigned to it because I used to have a Thompson submachine gun and that goes with the jeep, but I've never driven it) and back it up to the bridge site to haul him off when he's freed. Meanwhile the men around him discover that he can be cut out of his boot, and they do that because there is no way that the slab can be broken up without dragging him down deeper into the vice. So at the cost of a boot that crisis is past. I don't recall anyone except the Captain mourning over those fancy boots.

Now the bridge. We aren't going to use a Bailey, for some reason that I've forgotten. We're going to make an H-10 model out of timbers a hundred yards to the left of the destroyed bridge. This is the kind of bridge you see on railroads, with stringers laid on piers made of timber. To make a pier you lay out the sleeper timber for the bottom and another timber for the top. You cut support timbers to fit between them, fitting into notches and spiked on but with the weight borne by compression. The support timbers are slightly splayed out at the bottom so that the pier is narrower at the top. You spike on cross braces and raise the pier. Then you lay timber stringers lengthwise across the abutments and piers, and lay cross planks as the floor of the bridge.

This one is a 10-ton model. It's designed to hold a load of that weight. And we have to work fast. Next day we're going to have important people crossing it: Generals Patton, Eisenhower, Bradley, and Hodges, Secretary of War Marshall, and a couple of others. We know this because Patton's jeep has come by to inspect the crossing (that man leaves as little to chance as he can).

We finish the bridge late in the afternoon. And then, from the far side, down the road comes our first customer, and he's a big one: a dragon wagon (a tank retriever) with a Sherman tank loaded on it. This is a lot more than the ten ton we built the bridge to carry. And he's coming across.

The bridge holds. It groans, we groan, but it holds. Next day the great men roll on across toward the front. We stand in appropriate awe, and some salute. And we move on.

1944. Was it Chartres? In the middle of a sleepy night, as our convoy rumbles on its dusty way, we enter a city. There is a full moon and we can see well enough so that our blackout discipline is not a problem. Then the truck passes in front of a huge cathedral with twin towers. There is an open area with a fountain in its middle. In the moonlight the stone is white and almost glowing, and it imprints on my retina. Then we roll on, and the night becomes routine again. Memory will always say, "Chartres."

> *1994: Katy and I approach Chartres. The twin spires of the famous cathedral thrust above the hill on which it sits and above the mass of city buildings. We drive on into town, getting more and more enmeshed in crowded streets and turns but always following the signs that indicate the cathedral. Finally we get quite near it and find parking.*

> *Katy and I walk toward the cathedral, taking pictures as we go. The open area in front of the cathedral is really open; it's a pit, and some kind of construction or excavation is going on. There are what look like*

old walls down there. If there was a fountain in front of the cathedral in 1944, it's gone now.

We walk farther and this huge cathedral (third largest in the world) becomes impossible to film in a single frame. Then there is a sickening slip and a crunch— my video camera's hand strap has come off and the camera has fallen to the pavement. The heavy battery takes the main jolt and parts of the battery hang out of the case. Then I notice that the viewfinder is a stub. The cap and the lens have come off and are lying on the ground. I pick them up and hope I've got them all, and stick them on. The shattered battery goes into a trash can. Is the camera dead? (Turns out, it isn't.)

We walk up to the portal of the cathedral and find an open door. We go in and find ourselves in the standard gloom and chill of a stone church. But it's not as dark as most, thanks to the 3000 square yards of stained glass windows.

Among other tourists of many countries we wander along the aisles after viewing the nave from the rear. We pass the altar and choir and round the apse at the far end before traversing the right aisle. The nave is the widest Gothic nave in the world, and it soars high above us. And in all directions, the windows.

Time is beginning to press us today. We aren't sure how long it is going to take to get to Fontainebleau. And my 1944 route through here is not very certain. Maintenon for sure, but after that, memory doesn't serve. So we cut across country willy-nilly toward Fontainebleau.

We are passing south of Paris and all roads lead there. We have to work across the web. Fortunately there are enough signs.

1944: We have had a bad day. There is a gas scare, the rumor that the Germans are using poison gas. All this

65

time we've carried gas masks but haven't had them out of their pouches since practice in basic training. Now it seems like we may need them. Some of us haven't shaved -- not that it matters much for most of us, young as we are. I've been coaxing along a skipper beard. Not good. A beard will defeat the seal of the gas mask against the face. So off will come the juvenile beard when we halt for the night. Then there is some air-to-ground combat up ahead, though it apparently is an American P-47 that is strafing and bombing. Anyhow, we're edgey.

Then we enter the woodsy area that foretells the royal forest that gave birth to Fontainebleau. I search but don't locate the stretch of road where Benedict made his famous speech in 1944.

1944: Now we approach Fontainebleau. We're about to enter the forested area, and we stop along the road for piss call. The vehicles close up and we get out.

There is a low bank on the right and when we stop we are beside a young French woman on a bicycle. The bicycle is the main transport medium in these days of gas shortage and the French people we see on the move are all on bicycles. It is not uncommon to see a young man pedaling with an old woman perched on the handlebars. Anyhow, this time it is a young woman, alone. We have been out of civilization for some time and we're a young bunch of bucks, and young women are exceptionally interesting to us.

The young woman wheels her bike up on to the bank beside the road and stands looking off in the opposite direction. She does her best to pretend that we aren't there. And she's beside Benedict's truck.

Benedict is a lusty young man from the Missouri Ozarks. He doesn't speak French, nor do any of us. So he speaks to the young woman in Ozark English. And he describes her in loving and complete detail and tells her how beautiful she is, and he describes exactly what he would like to do about it. We are in the depths of France and no one speaks English, so he gets quite graphic. We never suspected that Benedict was that eloquent and imaginative.

Break is over, and the call comes to "load up and move out."

Benedict settles behind the wheel of his truck and fires up. Then the young woman turns, flashes a brilliant smile to him, and says in perfect English, "Sergeant, you have a vivid imagination!" And Benedict nearly drives over the truck in front of him getting out of there.

We bivouac a couple of miles down the road and the story gets around that the young woman is the daughter of the local English teacher. Could be. It makes the story even better.

My incipient beard comes off that evening and a couple of days later we find out that there is no substance to the gas rumor.

1994: Katy and I pass through some fairly solid park-like forest, and enter a city. And we find that memory has been faulty on a couple of counts: Fontainebleau is a pretty big city, and it isn't actually on the Seine River. It is not difficult to find the center of town, though the traffic is a bit heavy, but neither is it difficult to overshoot the town center. We park off the street under some trees and quickly find our hotel.

A young woman behind the desk responds to our tentative French by speaking good English. Yes, she's expecting us. She smiles, and I recognize her. Actually, I recognize her grandmother, or all the grandmothers of all current French girls. Still, it is nice to imagine that this one's grandmother was that beautiful girl at Le Rove; she was from southern France, at any rate, we find out. Later she turns on her special smile, the one she reserves for old geezers, and the day stays bright for an hour.

The hotel is a block from the palace. We settle into a spacious, well-furnished room, which is incidentally *the least expensive real hotel room we find in France (about $40). Then we go for a walk in the formal garden of the palace, a palace that never entered our imagination in 1944.*

This leads us farther into the hunting lodge cum palace. We enter from the garden side. (The garden is more like a park, with rigidly trimmed trees that look like upside down ice cream cones, and several pools, the large one at least 300 yards on the side. All the trees are trimmed and disciplined so severely that you can hear them squeak in agony, Katy says.) A break in the high wall of the palace complex leads us past a gate with the Oval Court to our left. This, with its large arched gate surmounted by busts, must be the formal entrance to the palace. On our right is a large cobble-stoned court, the Cour Henri IV, where the carriages from Paris would no doubt debauch and unload (I suppose that the royalty would continue across to the Cour Oval).

We continue around the wing of the palace, and come round into the Jardin de Diane. This, the Garden of Dianna, faces the city. On our left is the wing with "H&D" monograms on the windows. Henri II of France installed them to honor his mistress, Diane of Piotiers. But the Dianna of the garden is a statue of Dianna the Huntress, accompanied by her stag. Four hounds sit below the statue, facing the compass points, and with streams of water arcing out from anatomically correct jets to make up the fountain. Pictures here are a must. Then the peacock squawks, and we locate him across the garden, spreading his tail and displaying for indifferent peahens.

We don't go into the hunting lodge/palace, because it's closing time. But on the closed end of the Garden of Dianna rises the quarter where Napoleon had his favorite home, and to which he sent his famous dispatch to Josephine, "Coming home. Do not bathe."

The custodian of the palace grounds calls out that the place is now closing, so we go back to our hotel. Supper is in the hotel dining room. This is our first sit-down, white-table-cloth French meal, and it's good. Service is attentive and unobtrusive.

I've brought along some packets of Minnesota wild rice, a scarce and expensive commodity in Europe. I give not only our compliments to the cook but also the wild rice, emphasizing that it's for her and the staff and not for guests. The gift seems to be well received. In my experience this gift never fails and it's worth the extra pounds in our luggage.

1944: Our mission in Fontainebleau is to replace a blown bridge across the Seine River. Memory says that the river here runs through a gorge and that it is a hundred yards wide. Memory, it will turn out fifty years later, is not perfect.

This is going to be hard. In the first place there is the rubble of the former bridge. But most of it has fallen away and our work now is mostly to clear and prepare the abutments. The Germans have made a bad mistake, too. They failed to blow the center pier and we can put a roller on it after we've prepared it. So now we have a place to halve the span.

However, the other problem is less tractable. On the near side the road approaches the bridge from a T-intersection that is so close to the abutment that we won't have room to build a long rear section to balance the bridge when, after assembling it, we want to roll it across the river. Behind the intersection is not only a brushy woods—that could be cleared away—but a hill that is too big a job to carve out under our deadline.

We have 200 men. We have enough bridge sections. We put the bridge panels and attachments together, and build a triple-wide (and therefore triple-weight) rear section for counter-balance and push the bridge across as we build it, moving panels back to the rear as they approach the near-shore rollers. It works. This is one bridge where almost everyone in the company works at the bridge site. By the end of the day the bridge is across and is carrying traffic. The bridgehead on the other side, fortunately, is unopposed. No German defense at this site.

1994: Before leaving town I want to find the bridge site where we put a Bailey across the Seine in one afternoon under difficult conditions. The city map indicates two places where the bridge could have been, neither of them actually in Fontainebleau. We head for the more promising one, not getting lost very often.

There it is. It has to be the one. It's inside a wide bend in the Seine, and the near approach ends in a "T" intersection. There has been a lot of change here, though. The intersection has been moved back and I don't recall that it was as big and busy a road as it now is. The woods behind the intersection, which in 1944 blocked us from building a proper counterpoise for the bridge as it was pushed out, have changed. They are all young, second growth; the larger trees are gone. And they're more open and park-like.

The river gorge is not as deep as memory says it was nor as wide, but you can't argue with geology. The center pier is there. The bridge, of course, is one that replaced our temporary Bailey long ago. But the general configuration was carried over to this new one. The near abutment has been built out into a sort of causeway that shortens the span to the center pier and the bridge fabric is neat and modern concrete. It carries a lot of traffic, even at this fairly early hour.

Satisfied, we continue on north toward Melun. We pass through the open forest that looks exactly like our 1944 bivouac area and it feels like home. It's typical European forest with mostly fairly large trees and with the undergrowth sparse and mostly consisting of ferns. There is no trash of fallen trees or limbs.

1944: We never actually see the city of Fontainebleau. After building the Fontainebleau bridge our company sets up bivouac in the woods between it and the town of Melun to the north. Somehow it feels just like the Louisiana maneuvers. The same tents, the same towering trees (but not longleaf pine this time). There is little underbrush.

We are here for some days. Life is still Spartan but there is nothing much to do. The world is concentrating on the liberation of Paris and the German opposition in this section is light. In the woods, it's quiet.

Late one afternoon two young women on bicycles pass by and they pause. They are prostitutes heading for work in Paris. I'm told that they speak either English or some universal language.

We cross the Seine at Melun. Before we do, we pass another place that looks like 1944. This is an open field on fairly low farmland with a line of woods beyond.

1944: We have moved on and here we are a few miles away, parked in an open field near Melun. The field seems to be fallow though some other fields carry mangles, those big woody members of the beet family that stand half out of the ground and are cut up for livestock feed.

For some unreasonable military reason we are camped about half a mile in front of a battery of 155 millimeter canon, Long Toms. They can hurl a shell six inches in diameter and 18 inches long for 20 miles and that's what they are doing over where we intend to sleep. The noise is terrific.

When a Long Tom goes off the first effect is a shock wave that, at half a mile, bats the clothes against your body. Then comes the crash of sound mingled with the rush of the shell going overhead. A couple of times a shell sheds its rotating band (a band of copper an inch wide that rings the shell and provides a soft "bite" on the grooves in the barrel). When a band breaks loose it screams through the air like a banshee. At dusk the blooms of flame from the muzzles light the area fitfully.

We have all dug shelter trenches to sleep in tonight. Mine is a bit shallow but not much of me sticks up above the surface. We don't turn in early because the noise of the canon is unsettling.

Then, after dark, we draw counter-battery artillery fire. A mobile German 88 has crept within range, and it's laying down a walking barrage to try to get the Long Toms. It starts in the field north of us and shot after shot lands. Each one has that whistling scream that the high-velocity 88 makes, a falling whistle. Each shell lands closer to us, as he methodically stitches across the field to try to find the Long Toms. And he's short! He's a half mile short! In fact, though he doesn't have the Long Toms' range, he does have ours. I go for my trench and can't find it in the dark. The shells are landing closer, coming right across our bivouac area. The incoming whistles are getting shorter and shorter (you don't get to hear the shell that lands right on you). I get down beside the rear tires of the air compressor truck. As Mauldin's Willie used to say, "I can't get no lower, Joe. Me buttons is in the way." I know that the next shell is going to land right on me. I'm wrong. It lands beyond me.

You learn to talk to God about your situation when that sort of thing happens. Earnestly.

The shell is on a low, flat trajectory and it skins between the wheels of one of the trucks. Dagger Wallace and a couple of other hardy souls have disdained to go to trenches and are sleeping in the cab of the truck. The shell digs a crater a few yards ahead of them. Other men, like Salisbury, are sleeping in the backs of trucks.

Another incident, also involving Dagger. We had found some German 20 mm shells a few days back, and got to figuring that they would make swell salt-and-pepper shaker souvenirs. Dagger and I each get a pair out of their casings, and go to work.

Getting the TNT out of the shell body is no great trick. It drops out after we unscrew the tracer plug. Then we find out which way the fuse that makes up the nose unscrews, and get that off.

Now we have the striker mechanism from the nose and a tetryl cap the size of a pencil eraser. That tetryl is fairly sensitive, but we have to get it out or give up the project. I soak mine in gasoline to loosen the red glue that holds it it, and carefully unscrew it; my shells are fully disarmed.

Dagger isn't as patient. He buries a fuse under about three inches of dirt to muffle the explosion and jabs it with his ever-handy knife. Three inches is not quite enough dirt. He picks little bits of aluminum cap casing out of his hands for weeks.

> *1994: Once across the Seine, Katy and I turn south toward Montereau. Nothing looks familiar. Time will not allow us to continue south to Pont sur Yohne, where the 537th built a bridge across the Yohne tributary to the Seine. We cut northeast toward Nogent sur Seine and Sezanne. Still nothing. We swing more northerly and reach Epernay.*

On we go, after the front moves again. Part of our unit builds a bridge over the Yohne to the south. We continue east, now going away from Paris, through Nogent-sur-Seine, turn toward the north and go through Sezanne. Things move faster now, and we pass through Epernay. The place is only a name. Few if any of our men know that this is prime champagne country and that some cellars hold vintages being saved for the German elite.

This is the heart of the champagne country. The vineyards are not a prominent feature of the landscape but there they are on every south-facing slope. This is nearly the northern limit of the wine country. We drive on through Epernay, passing up its champagne tours.

 1944: We approach Reims at dusk. The squared-off cathedral stands silhouetted on the horizon, a red glow behind it shining through its narrow windows. There are no tall buildings near it. The red glow is not sunset, which would be west of us. It must be a burning city. Actually, the cathedral itself was burned, but its main treasures were saved.

1994: Reims—"Ranz" as they nasally call it in French. As the city comes into view, the skyline sight is the dark bulk of the cathedral, its square twin towers to the left. Most of the cathedral rises above the city, just as it did in 1944. The foreground buildings, however, are different. On the left outskirts of the city are white grain elevators, and the city has spread greatly. But there's no mistaking the cathedral.

Again we drive into a city that is ringed by modern suburbs but has an old core. In the middle of that core is a hill, and on its crest is the cathedral.

The cathedral (in 1994) is fully restored on the inside, but has some scaffolding on the facade. In the First World War it was badly bombarded and was rebuilt with American funds. The square across the street from the cathedral is named "Place Carnegie" and I suppose that's in recognition of the big contributor.

For a change this cathedral has a wide street with parking spaces that leads up to the portal. Katy and I park only three blocks away and walk up the slight incline. The sky is threatening rain.

There are a lot of people visiting this "national" church. Here, in 496, the Frankish (Germanic) king Clovis was baptized, beginning France's conversion to Christianity. That church is long gone, of course, and the present church dates only from just before 1300. All the kings of France, from Louis VII in 1137 to Charles X in 1825, were anointed here. It is here also that the Dauphin was conducted by Joan of Arc to be reluctantly crowned, saving France as a nation. So the French are sentimental about this cathedral, and most of the tourists are French, unlike at other famous sites in France.

Other members of the Company will remember Reims for another reason. Here they do find the champagne cellars.

Inside, this cathedral is less cold and dank than the others. Part of this is due to the high, narrow nave that feels less like a cave, and part is due to the discreet artificial lighting. The stained glass here is less prominent than at Chartres, maybe because the aisles are lit by narrower windows.

Along the bases of columns on the inside of the right aisle there are high-impact scars in the stone. They are about a foot across and center on deep pits where the stone is crushed. Only shrapnel or direct hits by bullets like .50 caliber will make those pits. These scars, more than anything else, show that the cathedral was so badly damaged in 1914-18. The restored stonework merges seamlessly into the oldest work, and the pitted stone was clearly left as a memorial.

Outside, the cathedral also looks fully ancient until you look closely. The statuary is mostly eroded with simple age, the stone melted by the elements so that features are blurred and rounded. But across the right tympanum are carvings of the men at work on the cathedral, and you notice that the blocks are separated by blank, flat stonework. These blocks were salvaged from the rubble, and not enough remained to fill the row. The scaffolding hides what is going on currently.

We find the public toilet (they're not too plentiful nor well marked in France), and then go to the semi-subterranean building beside the cathedral that *housed the treasury. The treasures that are reported to be there (a 12th century chalice used in communion by the French kings, and Charlemagne's talisman which he believed to contain a piece of the true cross) are not on display.*

As we have found in all the cathedrals we've visited, there is no admission charge in spite of the guidebook's statement that admission is over three dollars.

Stalemate at the West Wall

1944: We run out of gas at Suippes. Patton has pulled all of his tricks to get Eisenhower to give him priority on gas, but we've overrun out supply line.

There is no front. The German lines are full of holes and our lines are a series of salients. Patton has taken an armored unit far beyond us, penetrating to the Saar Valley beyond Metz. He thinks that he could push to the Rhine if he only had enough gas. He's wrong. The terrain beyond there is not fit to carry armor, and the Siegfried Line is intact. All of us now settle down for supplies to catch up.

The country here is still pocked with the shell holes of World War I. An apparently true story is that one GI, a veteran of WWI, took shelter in the same shell hole he used 28 years earlier.

It's a spooky time. At night on guard duty some of us see drifting shadows slipping along the edges of the woods. No point in raising an alarm. It's just forlorn Germans trying to rejoin their army. The debris of a rout is scattered about. There is a German field kitchen, with iron wood-fired stove in a horse-drawn wagon. I pick up a pair of horse goggles, hemispheres of clear plastic designed to be tied onto a horse to keep the dust out of its eyes.

One day, I'm playing with an old French sword-bayonet, one of those slim, 20-inch things that can be used on a rifle or by hand. I mention to Benedict that in the old days the skill of a swordsman was demonstrated by his catching a tossed finger ring on the point of his sword. Without a word, Benedict pulls off a ring and tosses it into the air. I catch it neatly and hand it back. Then he wants to see me do that again. I know better.

We nearly lose the air compressor truck here. I've got a big German flare pistol, about 12 gauge, loaded with a magnesium flare. I've taken out the flare, poured in extra powder, and replaced the flare. At close range this is an awesome defensive weapon. Anyhow, I keep it in the cab of the truck. One of our men is fooling around the cab and I warn him not to touch the pistol. I get about 50 feet away and there is a "Boom!" behind me. I run back, and there he is, bouncing on one foot and with his tongue stuck out sideways, spraying a fire extinguisher on a bright white flame lodged in one of the sandbags on the floor of the truck cab. We just have to let it burn out. Magnesium burns at 2000 degrees, and you can't drown it. And there are a dozen boxes of machine gun ammunition plus four boxes of hand grenades in that cab. I get rid of the pistol.

1994: Katy and I drive on to Verdun. We didn't see much of the city in 1944, as usual; we were routed around cities when possible. Its setting is the Meusse River valley and it isn't very visible from the surrounding highlands. The city of Verdun itself is unremarkable as we roll on through.

Both of us want to see the WWI memorials, especially the Ossuary. It was here that Marshall Petain called a halt to the German advance, drew the line at the Meusse, and said, "Il ne passe pas, They shall not pass." Thousands of men died in the trenches here -- the "small" American cemetery alone holds 15,000 graves.

Past Verdun and up the hill, and we find the sign that points down the road to the left to the Museum and Ossuary. It leads on through the woods, winding as it goes. I look for any place that could resemble our Verdun campsite, but no luck. As we go on, the old shell craters and the zigzag, grass-covered lines of trenches show where the WWI stands were made. The trees are all under 70 years old because the shelling here had completely denuded the land. On our left is the marked site of a destroyed village with the locations of homes signposted; there is nothing but holes.

We emerge from the woods and at an intersection is a memorial to the desperate stand of the British here. On a stone plinth lies a dead or dying lion, collapsed as only Rodin could carve it. Ahead is the Verdun Museum.

We go into the Museum even though the guard points out that we will only have fifteen minutes before they close. The salvaged battlefield debris has been assembled into a recreation of the trench area, with raw earth plowed into heaps by the shelling. Along the surrounding corridor there are 1918 trucks, guns, field equipment.

Then we continue toward the Ossuary, visible on its hill about a mile away. A low, semi-gothic arch in side profile and over 150 yards long, the main hall sits crosswise on the hill with a blunt pointed tower like an upended artillery shell over its center entrance. Inside are the thousands of bones of unidentified soldiers, recovered on the battlefield and with no regard to nationality. The whole building is packed with bones. I decline to go in. Katy goes in for the brief time allowed before closing.

On the slope in front of the Ossuary the crosses of 16,000 graves stand in geometric precision. As we get ready to return to the main road the big iron bell of the Ossuary begins to toll. Its tone has been selected to perfectly typify Poe's description: "Hear the tolling of the bells -- iron bells! What a world of solemn thought their monody compels! ... For every sound that floats From the rust within their throats Is a groan."

1944: I'm riding shotgun on the ration truck, so this must be while we're camped east of here and after the bridge at Arneville. We pass on various days through towns whose names I recall from WWI stories: Mars-la-Tour, St. Mihel, Bar-le-Duc. On one of the trips to find the ration point Parker (who's driving) and I pass below a hillside covered with thousands of white crosses. On top of the hill is a concrete building, long and low and set crosswise, with a blunt tower. I know that this is the Verdun cemetery, because I know that much about WWI history. We don't stop.

1094: Katy and I are going to strike straight toward Metz, so that we can check into our hotel before supper. That means that we leave the strict following of the 1944 route. Between Verdun and Metz the road is not only unfamiliar but also not very interesting.

1944: All the roads in this area are familiar to two of us. Riding on the ration truck every day, often without knowing just where the ration point is, Parker and I cover a swath that changes as our bivouac and the ration point change.

A familiar sight on the road is the Red Ball Express. This is a fleet of trucks, each with a red circle painted on its bumper. The Red Ball Express has absolute right of way and they drive as fast as they can. They are the supply line.

One day near Thiaucourt our ration truck gets caught in a Red Ball Express convoy. Fast as they drive, Parker drives faster and he wants to pass. No go. They won't move over for him. One of them moves into the center of the road so we can't pass. So Parker hooks the right front corner of our truck rack (I'm sitting beside it) on the left rear corner of his rack, and guns the motor. We pass. And ever after, the rack of our truck sits a little askew.

Two or three times, in our ramble over south Lorraine and north Alsace, we meet the famous Patton jeep. It is always traveling toward the front; Patton flies back from these trips and sends back the jeep with its flashy equipment stowed, so as to give the right image. The stories about the man are true. His helmet is polished and gleaming. On each front fender of the jeep is a huge chrome plated siren with a red light in its front. A .50 caliber machine gun is mounted on a center post (if you fired it sideways, it would roll the jeep over), and an air-cooled .30 caliber machine gun is mounted on a post by his right hand. He sits so that the pearl handle of his right revolver is visible. When we meet Patton, Parker says, "Salute! Salute!" and I don't. Not because I don't respect the man, but because I can get away with it.

1994: Katy and I approach Metz, dropping down into the Moselle Valley (to use the French spelling) along a fairly steep and curvy road under the brow of the headland where Fort Driant sat. There are now suburbs to cross, and the modern map shows that the entire valley from Luxembourg to Nancy is now an urban corridor. Then across the river into Metz, noting that the city is indeed set (in its riverward side) on a series of islands in the river. This section of the Moselle is full of islands, as we found to our sorrow in 1944.

1944: The battle for Metz is one of the toughest since Normandy. The city and its environs has been a tough nut to crack for centuries, and it's in the way of any army trying to go east or west through this region.

The Germans have set up the Moselle River as a line to be held. The history books will say little about this, but one book will be written about "*The Forgotten Battle*" giving details that square with our memory.

We are all held up here for weeks while the line is contested. Even after the nut has been cracked and we are heading north into Luxembourg, the forts of Driant and St. Jean will hold out, safe behind their sixteen feet of reinforced concrete.

At one point some of our men will be welding up beehive charges to blow through the concrete. These charges are welded up out of sheet metal into a sort of hatbox shape, except that the "business" side is a hollow cone, a Monroe charge. When filled with Composition C (later to be known as plastique) and exploded, the hollow cone focuses the blast into a concentrated line of power that can punch through several feet of concrete. Even stacked two high, these charges aren't enough to punch through those forts. We understand that the forts only give up when gasoline is poured into their ventilators and ignited.

Probably in connection with the Monroe charges, one of our platoons goes onto the grounds of Fort Driant during the day -- the nights belong to the Germans. Jefferson notes a motorcycle in one of the buildings and plans to take it with him the next day. In the morning of the next day he finds a dead German straddling the cycle – it was boobytrapped.

1995: The Metz railway station itself is of the older European architectural style, long and low and stone-faced. For that matter, this whole section of the city is of 1890s to 1920s architecture. There is no sign of the destruction that had to accompany WWI and WWII, when Metz was hotly contested.

As the Romans noted, Metz is a natural fortress in a strategic junction of Europe. It has been fought over and, almost without exception, has held out under assault. It was a pivotal stronghold in WWI and I recall the pictures in our family's old "World War" book of the 1920s showing the Barking Turtle of Metz. This was a smooth quarter-sphere of steel and concrete when retracted, but shaped like a piston that could be elevated. Then a short canon would drop into firing position, and the Turtle would become a rotating pillbox that could fire and then retract. What I do not know in 1944 is that the Barking Turtles are still there, and still operational. They have been neglected and their ammunition is old but some of them are actually used by the Germans for close-quarters defense of fortifications.

1994: At the end of the railway complex is the German Gate, a tower in the ancient Metz city wall that was so named because it was the perennial route of German invasions. I picked up a postcard picture of it in 1944, naturally with a German label

82

that called it the "Deutches Tor." Anyhow, now it looks a little different from the 1944 picture, and it's named "La Port des Allemandes." Who knows what incarnation it is in now, having been first set up by the Romans and probably damaged in every war since then.

1944: When our company finally comes through the city of Metz after our time in the woods west of here and our time in places like Euvazin and Pont-a-Mousson, we are briefly billeted in a German military building. The streets are littered with unburied German dead and some of them have been dead too long. Metz in 1944 is not a pleasant city. You wonder how the civilians fared; we don't see many of them. Maybe they have learned to avoid uniforms, maybe the residents of this city have become Germanized in the 28 years since WWII.

After the war starts to move again, when the supply line has caught up with us, the 537th moves closer to the Moselle and to Metz. We are just out of range of the big guns, so our bivouac is safe.

However, some of our men are not. While we are camped in the woods, at a place that has no name in memory, some of the men are at the Moselle trying to put up a couple of bridges.

I'm still attached to the air compressor truck with my machine gun. Things are dull and I want one of my cartridges as a souvenir. It isn't hard to work out the bullet and dump the powder. But the primer is a different matter. There is no way to remove it, and no safe way to explode it. Finally, I load it into the chamber, grab the D-handles, and push the butterfly trigger with my thumbs. POW! even the primer on one of those cartridges packs as much punch as a small rifle bullet. But no one comes to investigate, and I get the souvenir (which will lie in a display case many years later).

It's been raining. We sleep in pup tents, each of two men furnishing half of the tent from his pack, and I draw C. C. Natvig as my partner. It is not much fun to live in a

83

pup tent on the ground and in the French mud when it rains. However, we had overrun a supply depot that had a stock of German snow troopers' coats, made of white sheepskin with the fur side inside. That inch thick pad of wool becomes my mattress. Later I'll ship it home with a French caplock muff pistol in each pocket, and use one sleeve to pad the box in which I ship my liberated German artillery binoculars.

Others aren't so fortunate with their souvenir coats. Gaskill is fined $25 (real money, in those days) for being "out of uniform" while wearing his. Technically, I suppose he *was* breaking some important military rule, being dressed in an enemy uniform. But we all think that the Army, as personified by our officers, is too pickey. No one would mistake Gaskill for a German soldier. At this stage of the war, no German soldier would laugh so easily -- and make others laugh -- the way Gaskill does.

The mud gets to us. French mud is deep and sticky. One of the men has a German flare pistol, firing a shell like a 12-gauge shotgun but with flares instead of shot. One of the shells is for practice in dodging artillery fire instead of for illumination, and the gun owner gets cute. We have all just gotten our chow and have our mess kits full while we locate places to sit and eat among the trees. The flare gun goes off, but we naturally don't know that that's what it is. All we know is that there is this whistle exactly like an incoming 88. We all hit the dirt -- the mud, that is.

Fortunately for him the perpetrator remains unknown long enough for us to cool down.

Another day in the woods, another carelessness. I have a .25 caliber automatic pistol and I let another man look at it. He rakes back the slide, loading a round. He's holding it by the grip, squeezing the safety, and with his finger on the trigger. It goes off, fortunately pointing at the ground. Such a small gun isn't loud, but we both disappear for a while.

1994: This morning, after a hotel breakfast Katy and I are going to take our separate ways. She will get her chance to walk after three days of nothing but riding and sightseeing and not enough exercise. I will get my chance to visit some WWII sites that are probably not meaningful to her.

All I have to do is get off the main road that wants to take me back to Verdun, and find the small road along the west bank of the Moselle. Another small detour through unwanted suburbs, and I'm on my way. It took an hour of driving to get out of town.

No time now to climb the heights to get onto the grounds of Fort Driant. Too bad. Local information is that the grounds are open to tourists, it being an obsolete military reserve. But in fact it's not open.

1944: Fort Driant is a real thorn in everyone's side. It sits on a bluff that overlooks the Moselle valley from Metz to out-of-sight south. All the possible sites for us to cross the river are within view of this fort (and of a couple of smaller forts across the river). That means that, when we try to build a bridge, we can be seen and shot at directly by high velocity artillery. Smoke screens help, but they don't always conceal. A couple of the nastiest river crossings in Europe are at Dornot and Arneville, south of Metz.

1994: Just before Ars, stone arches lift beside the road, labeled "aqueduc romain." It's part of the Roman aqueduct that used to bring water to the city of Metz. We didn't see this one in 1944, or at least I didn't. Stonework that lasts 2000 years, through wars and removal of stones for local building, is pretty durable stuff.

Then I come to the village of Dornot, a quarter mile to the right and back from the road I'm on.

1944: Dornot is a disaster. The US forces don't actually lose ground here but gains have to be given up at considerable cost. An engineer outfit that tries to put up a treadway (floating) bridge suffers 50% casualty. Our platoons get assault bridges down to the crossing. An infantry battalion gets across, and finds that the stream that they crossed is only a channel of the Moselle, and they're on an island. Without necessary armor support, the troops have to pull back. I'm not at that crossing, and the men who were aren't articulate at the time about what happened. I will get the straight story from Salisbury many years later.

1994: Dornot is a small cluster of homes and the inevitable bakery. The street up from the Moselle-side road is narrow and it isn't straight, and within the town it begins to steepen. Then it becomes really steep, so that my little car labors in second gear. It's narrow and stone walls grow on both sides. It turns right about half way up the hill, maybe 100 feet above the village roofs, beside a vinyard. I stop there to take some pictures.

The road winds down to the curve, apparently concealed from Fort Driant and even from the forts directly across the river. But from where I stand I can see the headland that carries Fort Driant, even though the mist today makes it too fuzzy to see details or accurately judge the distance. The stone walls give some cover for the next few yards, and then it's sitting-duck country. Artillery at Fort Driant can fire with direct observation, and the range is easy.

The road then goes down into the village and back to the north-south road. Beyond that is the railway embankment that offered some shelter in 1944, then the river flats. They're wooded now, and may have been the same then. It's low ground, it looks boggy, and I wouldn't want to build a bridge there. Further, what looks like the river is actually only one of the channels, and beyond is an island with the main channel yet to be crossed. If I were under military pressure enough to make me willing to lose a lot of men, then I'd try to cross here; not otherwise.

1944: The job of the 537th at Dornot is to supply assault boats for the river crossing. I'm not there, since this only involves one of our platoons. My information comes from the later report of Salisbury and from the book about the Metz crossings.

None of us know it, but the Army is operating on flawed information. The river here looks like a simple proposition and the maps that are available don't give enough detail. The result is that our infantry is sent to cross a simple river and in reality they find that they've crossed onto an island and that there is a bigger channel ahead of them.

The crossing is chaotic. Our platoon gets onto that narrow road between the stone walls, heading down to the river with the assault boats. They run into a traffic jam. There are tanks beside the road and traffic ahead is at a standstill. German artillery is probing for range through the smoke screen. Our men get some boats delivered, but not all can get through.

Then the smoke blows away and the German guns get the range. A tank is hit. Our platoon has to dump the boats where they are in order to clear the road. They have to turn around where there is no room to turn. One of them bends the tongue of his trailer and has to lope home with the trailer trotting sidewise like a dog. None of our men is hit, but the infantry takes a beating and has to withdraw from the island next day in the face of a German counterattack.

1994: Back to the road, and south again. Noyeant sur Moselle, and then Arneville.

Arneville is where the Rupt de Mad, a moderate stream, flows into the Moselle. The valley of the Rupt de Mad comes from the west, but it curves so that most of it is north-flowing.

*The road makes a curve away from the Moselle here,
crosses the Rupt de Mad on a concrete bridge, and
then curves back toward the river. Most of Arneville
is on that curve and it's almost entirely residential.
An older couple is in their yard and I ask them about
a bridge, a "pont militaire." They've never heard of it,
but they've lived here only 30 years or so. Well, it
almost certainly was on the site of that newer
concrete bridge.*

1944: Arneville is costly to the 537th. The military
historian who will write the only book on the Metz
campaign will comment on the kind of courage that it
takes for an Engineer, unarmed and unable to shoot
back, to sit twelve feet up in the air tightening bolts on a
bridge that's inching across a stream under fire. The
standard orders, when a bridge is to be built to support a
crossing like this, includes "at any cost."

Again, I am back at the forest bivouac while some of our
platoons work on the Arneville crossing, not sorry to
miss this one.

The engagement at Arneville takes several days. On
two successive nights, Jefferson swims across under
phosporus shell fire to take a line over to make a ferry.

Part of our company is working in an exposed area,
under direct fire, for 12 hours. By some miracle, no one
is hit -- at first.

The air compressor truck is at Arneville. Why am I not?

My gun has been transferred to the ration truck, and I
with it. This is partly in response to the fact that, when
the air compressor is working at a bridge site, I'm
supernumerary and not needed. But there's another
reason. One of the men in the kitchen crew, Pauley, has
requested front-line work, and I'm traded for him.

A couple of years later, in a college Freshman English
class, I will write of this episode:

His first name? I never did know it,

And don't think it makes any difference.
We just called him "Pauley, the cook,"
A quiet, composed, and thoroughly straightforward
    fellow.
We ran out of gas east of Reims, the whole army,
And there our mail finally found us.

He told me that night what his letter
Had said -- his third brother missing in action.
That got him. We tried to dissuade him
From sticking his neck out and leaving the kitchen
To work on the line building bridges.
No use, He knew what the score was,
A Jap was the same as a German.

We moved on, and there on the Moselle
An infantry bridgehead was cut off without antitank
    guns.
A bridge must be built in a hurry, a Bailey,
In spite of the heavy bombardment from Metz up the
    river.
We built it. The records say no, but we built it
And paid for it too -- ten men and two officers
    wounded,
Nordlund, who died the next day -- and Pauley.
A hole in his forehead with white showing through
Was the only mark on him.

We brought back his helmet for salvage
And turned in his bag to Supply
And someone who lived near his home town
Promised to bring back the story.
The authorities sent home a wire,
"... regret to inform you ..."

Now, in the poem I'll take some poetic liberty, mixing
Dornot and Arneville.

The real story of Pauley's death, according to Salisbury,
who was there, is that the men worked most of the day
with no casualties, though they were under fire all the

time. Then a heavy salvo came in. Pauley dived for cover beside a stack of wood, and chose the wrong side of the stack. An 88 came in, hit the wood and failed to explode, and ricocheted into Pauley. It was like being hit by a bullet over three inches in diameter. Pauley died instantly.

Nordlund, as I mentioned in the poem, died the next day. I think that it was his helmet that I saw. Ten others were wounded, some seriously. It was the worst day for the 537th in the whole war.

I will often wonder what would have happened if we hadn't been traded. Would Pauley be writing a memoir?

> *1994: Between the main road and the river rises a high railway embankment. Beside the Rupt de Mad it is pierced by a viaduct that takes a dirt road toward the river. After looking about in the town and not seeing anything left of 1944, I drive down that dirt road.*
>
> *It goes a way, curves, and gives off to a smaller dirt road to the right that passes under another square viaduct through another railway embankment. Maybe this is the way. The road dead-ends at a sort of rubble dump in the marshy area just beyond. The delta of the Rupt de Mad is flat, low ground that would be a problem for heavy military vehicles. There is nothing to see here either.*

1944: After the action at Dornot and Arneville our Company is moved to an actual village, Euvazin. This is a standard Eastern French village, untouched by the war that has bypassed it and inhabited by its regular people. We get billeted in real houses. My platoon is in the Mayor's residence, an old manor house that has seen a lot of use.

> *1994: Back to Arneville, and up the valley, along a good road that will lead to Mars-la-Tour, except that I'm turning off and taking the smaller road (still well surfaced) that leads to Thiaucourt.*

There, I seek out a still smaller road that will take me to the little town of Euvazin. A few miles farther, and there it is.

The road I was on ran along a high ground, and the stub road to Euvazin goes down into a valley, the same valley of the Rupt de Mad, which here nearer its source is a little stream.

1944: Walking along the streambed in Euvazin, upstream from the bridge, with the stream a trickle in this dry tag-end of summer, I find a dud 37 millimeter shell from WWI lying in the gravel. You don't pick up duds, but it's harmless, so I leave it. The east of France is full of leftover trash of war. For well over 50 years France will have bomb-disposal squads combing the country for unexploded ordinance of both wars.

1994: The road to the village passes over a railway on a fairly high bridge. I park the car in the access road of the fields to the left, and get out. The railway has been electrified now, and the rail cut is a bit more aged and overgrown. But I can still see, down near the track level, outcrops of the fossil bearing rock.

1944: A rock outcrop is always interesting. I get down into the railway cut, though it is a tough climb, and poke about in the eroded rock. Sure enough, there are fossils. It's impossible for me to estimate the era, with fossils that are different from what I've pulled out of the Ordovician of home, but they're good. There are lots of well preserved brachiopods and bryazoans. But the prizes are echinoderms, here the shells of round sea urchins. One large one, some three inches across, still has the Aristotle's lantern, the five-tooth jaw. And there are three small ones, each a half inch across, so perfect that under magnification you can see the pores in the madroporite. I gather a small handful and, when opportunity presents, I send a little box of them home. Most of the fossils will go to children and grandchildren, but the three little echinoderms will stay with me for the next fifty years.

To the left of the road is where our latrine was positioned. First comes a small field, now green with some forage crop, then a line of bushes, then the latrine field. There is nothing there now; the land is fallow.

1944: Ah, the latrine field. Backed by a row of bushes that screens it from the road, we have taken a flat-bottomed wooden assault boat and overturned it. Then we cut two holes in the bottom, and have the first comfortable sit-down latrine in our tour.

And one morning I'm sitting there, doing my duty, when one of the local young ladies walks by. She says, "Bon jour, M'sieur!" and I say "Bon jour, Mam'selle!" and life goes on. Both of us are pretty blasé about it all.

Beyond that, the hill falls away into the valley, and the railway continues on across its own arched stone viaduct across the Rupt de Mad, and picks up on the other side of the valley. As I stand looking, finding everything essentially unchanged here, the chug of a farm tractor emerges from Euvazin and heads for where I am. I go back to the car, get in, and cross the bridge over the railway into town.

This village is unchanged from 1944. The same squared and largely blank building walls rising directly beside the road, the same gray-brown color of the buildings. Even the size of the village is the same.

At the "L" turn of the street to the left in town center, the local manor home and mayor's house are exactly where they were, exactly as they were. No one is about. The village seems deserted, just like other French villages.

1944: You recall that some of us are billeted in the manor home. I will have good reason to remember this place even after we move on; beside the front door is a sort of hall seat, and on it is a pad, about 18 inches wide and five feet long and over an inch thick. This will become my mattress for the next few months, until we get real beds at the end of the campaign. Looting? perhaps. I think of it as living off the land.

The manor home is not fancy, but there is a stone staircase inside. The place must be fairly old, because the stone steps are worn into deep hollows, almost into a ramp in the middle.

Turning left, I go down the street toward the bridge over the Rupt de Mad. Door stoops arise directly from the edge of the street, the uniform gray-brown plastered fronts of the houses, mostly blank.

1944. It's evening, or at least dusk. I will not remember why I go up up to the door and knock; I have some business with the local people, I guess. Anyhow, a woman opens the door and greets me. Instinctively. Her right hand goes up in a salute, and she starts to say, "Heil Hi---." And stops in confusion. People have been conditioned to, or perhaps they even want to, make the Hitler salute. Several years of occupation will do that to you. I make no comment, and she recovers.

Across the low bridge to the tee intersection against the valley side that marks the limit of the village, and along the dirt road to the left. Ahead is the railway bridge over the valley, to the left is the meadow across the stream where we parked our trucks.

The meadow is also one of our night guard posts. Two scenes will imprint.

First episode: it's late at night, and I'm alone in the meadow, probably on guard. From over the hill to the west comes a rattling roar, and a small formation of fighter bombers pass over. It's too dark to see them clearly, but the sound is not quite the loose rattle that a B-25 makes. They must be A-20s, fighter bombers designed for night fighting. I'd thought that they were obsolete.

Second episode: sitting in the cab of the air compressor truck "standing" guard about 2 o'clock in the morning.

93

Then I realize that Cornell is talking to me. He's come to relieve me, and he's found me sleeping. Here in a combat zone, that's a capital offense. Good thing it was Cornell and not the officer of the guard.

1994: I drive the barely passable road under the railway arches and turn around. This is Euvazin. It is exactly like the Euvazin of 1944.

There is no one to talk to, so I drive out and back to the main road, back to Thiaucourt. There isn't time to cut directly down to Pont-a-Mousson as I had intended. i have to go right back to Arneville and north to Metz if I'm going to get back at the time Katy and I had set for rendezvous.

1944: The 537th leaves Euvazin and goes on to a couple more towns. Then we end up at Pont-a-Mousson. Our billet is next to a burned-out bayonet factory. I pick up a couple of unscorched German bayonets. They turn out to be perfect throwing knives, able to punch through a door and tempered so that they don't break under such impact. American bayonets are forged steel, but more brittle. Two of them will be sent home.

We also overrun a doll factory of sorts, and someone picks up some parts.

Now, Stiff is a man who has to be seen to be appreciated. He's a good-natured grouser, one of our oldest men, able to grin lop-sidedly as he complains that army stew is made out of eyeballs and foreskins. Biding my time, I finally get to serve hash on the chow line when Stiff comes through with his mess kit. I manage to top a scoop of hash with an upward-staring glass doll's eye. You can hear Stiff on the other side of the river.

Bed-check Charlie quit flying over Pont-a-Mousson the night before we got there. Charlie is any German observation plane that comes over after dark, because we have air superiority such that daylight flights are out of the question. Someone set up an American 90 mm antiaircraft gun, and waited. One round, and Bed-check Charlie came down in flames.

1994: Traffic is lighter than at rush hour, and I find the hotel without any false turns. Katy is waiting, having just gotten back from her own foot journey through the tangle of Metz's streets, and we check out of the hotel.

We cut out of town to the east, our way-finding helped by the knowledge of the city I picked up reluctantly earlier this morning. Then across the superhighway and northeast toward Boulay and thence toward Saarlouis on the Saar River. It's a fairly long drive. The border between France and Germany is only an empty customs checkpoint, with nothing eventful to see until the edge of the Saar valley.

Between Upper Felsberg and Lower Felsberg, the road makes a sharp jog to the right and then to the left in order to drop diagonally down the valley wall. This jog is remembered by those of the 537th who found that the second curve exposed their right flanks to the defenders of the Saar valley. Katy and I park off the curve, listen to the busy traffic, and shoot some pictures.

1944: Even while Metz is being reduced, and later when the Moselle has been breached at places like Pont-a-Mousson, part of our company is working the Saar River. Again, and not to my sorrow, I'm not at this bridge site, because I'm now riding shotgun on the ration truck with Joe Parker as driver.

Reports coming back from this crossing tell of pretty stiff opposition. One of our men's duties is to bring assault boats down to the crossing so that the infantry can be ferried across. The men who worked on the Saarlautern crossing have cause to remember it. The fire is pretty heavy here also, though we don't lose any men killed. Some shrapnel wounds, one severe enough to send one of the men home. The stories coming back from this

95

place are more confused and obscure than those from Arneville. I do not regret not taking part in this one.

1994: Katy and I had planned to find the bridge and ferry site at Saarlouis, formerly Saarlautern. The landmark smokestack is gone; there is a smokestack, but it's in the wrong place. As for the rest, the area of the Saar is as built-up now as was the area of the Moselle. (Here, in Germany, that river is called the Mosel.) We cross the Saar and drive around a bit. For one thing, we're looking for a toilet, and not finding one. There is a public building in a park, but it's locked. Well, there are woods down the road.

We drive north along the Saar, noting that it is a well domesticated river, canalized with hardened banks. It wasn't that way in 1944.. We do find some woods, and answer the call of nature in the natural European style, and continue. Everything along the river is modernized and rebuilt. There can't be a single old landmark along here, so we cruise along toward Merzig and Metlach. When we pass close to the river, we can see some long barges under tow. The other boats are pleasure cruisers.

Beyond Merzig the road swings away from the river and up over a steep hill. The hill is the high headland along the river, which here has cut a deep cleft in the red quartzite. One wonders why the road can't just keep on beside the river, and has to go a few hundred feet up onto a hill. Then the hill drops down toward Metlach, and there's the river again.

There we cross to the west side, and climb up out of the valley again. We get up onto the top, and find that a big section of forest is being cleared for chalet-styled apartment blocks. A large residential and commercial development is under way. We drive just past that, and turn left onto an obscure road. I want Katy to see one of the scenic wonders of the area.

We didn't see this sight in 1944, but in 1987 my first wife Bernice and I had followed a notation on the Michelin map and found it. The road goes into the woods and ends in a big parking lot (with toilets). Then a path continues into the woods to a small park building with a porch. We appreciate the porch, because the mist is threatening to turn into rain.

This is The Cloeff. The hill falls away below us for over 500 feet, with just enough of the trees cleared out to enhance the view. There is the Saar River. It comes in a deep gorge from Merzig on our right, turns in a hairpin curve right below us, and exits in another deep gorge on the left. The river runs straight toward us for maybe three miles (it's lost in the mist) and runs away equally straight, precisely parallel to its right course, until it again disappears in the misty distance. And that, of course, is the reason why the road from Merzig to Metlach goes up over that hill—to avoid a ten-mile detour.

As we stand there drinking in the scene, the rain becomes definite. A long barge tow comes down the river on the arm to our right. Then our solitude is interrupted by the first of a small busload of German tourists who have come for the same view, and we walk back to the parking lot.

And this is why the housing development is going in. The very isolation and quiet and hushed forest setting is being destroyed so that it can be enjoyed. "They pave paradise, put up a parking lot," as the song says. The world is the same all over, but we have seen The Cloeff before it's drowned in apartment buildings.

Now we strike cross-country toward Luxembourg, due northwest. The afternoon is mostly spent, but the distances here are smaller than we Americans are used to.

Luxembourg

1944. North on the Moselle from Metz, our unit is moved to places like Thionville. There is no evident reason for moving north like this, and we all know that something is going to happen in the north but we have no idea what it will be. The history books will say that the Battle of the Bulge was a complete surprise to the US, but for the next 64 years I will have a gnawing doubt. If no one knew that the Bulge was coming, why were troops moved north to its southern flank? Rational people will point out that the Siegfried Line east of the Saar was particularly strong, but in that case why was so much effort put into crossing the Saar? And we see no evidence that the assault through the Saar valley is not successful. It is certain that we know, in 1944, that big action is waiting to the north.

At any rate, we head north from the Mosel valley into Luxembourg. We're going to be billeted at the village of Dalheim, southeast of Luxembourg City, but as usual we don't know anything about where we will stop.

1994: Katy and I enter Luxembourg through another of those abandoned border posts, empty thanks to the European Community. In short order we pass the turn-off to Dalheim and enter Luxembourg City from the south.

1987: Bernice, my first wife, and I are arriving in Luxembourg City to drive some of my 1944-45 route in Germany. We go to the tourist office and ask for some directions. The woman behind the counter asks if we've been in the city before, and I acknowledge my military visit. The woman becomes effusive and loads me with thanks, almost coming around the counter to kiss me. The Luxembourgers are genuinely grateful for our liberation of their country from the Germans. They don't like Germans much, even though German is one of the country's three official languages, together with French and

Letzenburgich. English, we find, is spoken by most Luxembourgers.

1994: At the tourist office Katy and I ask for help and are given the city's hotel directory. The information attendant is still happy to see a former GI, though not so effusively as the attendant in 1987. There are two hotel areas: the area near the station and the area up in the old city. Prices in the old city, where the new hotels are, will be much higher, and I already know the station area from previous trips. We settle on the Hotel Axe and trudge the two blocks to it. It is a small hotel set into the line of buildings, and we get a room immediately. It turns out to be small and otherwise unsatisfactory, and the desk clerk has us look at the room across the hall. This is better, but still not one of our best. Never mind, we can sleep anywhere and we take it.

With our car parked in the long term lot of the station, we turn in for the night.

1944: We are just a day short of Dalheim, the town where we'll spend most of our time in Luxembourg, and I've ridden shotgun on the ration truck to the ration point. It isn't at Esch yet, but the location will be forgotten. It is fairly early in the morning, because we try to get rations early, especially since we sometimes have to search for the ration point. A truck comes in from the 10th Armored Division, and the news is bad. They suffered heavy casualties last night in a major German counterattack. We don't know it immediately, but the Battle of the Bulge has begun.

Our unit continues north, and after passing through the southern edge of Luxembourg City, we turn southeast and settle at Dalheim.

Two items burn into visual memory in that brief pass through the city. One is a couple of cases of Coke being unloaded on a sidewalk; we haven't seen Coke since we left England. The other is the spectacular bridges of

Luxembourg City, great but slender arches thrown across the canyon that surrounds the old city.

1994: The night has been rough. I sleep well enough, but the street noise has badly disturbed Katy's sleep. The windows are single glazed and not too tight, and every street sound comes in full blast. It seems like all the trucks between Germany and Belgium drive down our street or next to it, and we have chosen a hotel in a district with a lot of nightlife. Loud arguments in the middle of the night are best tolerated with a switched-off hearing aid (such as I have, and Katy doesn't). We are intending to stay in the city one more night. Some changes will have to be made.

Luxembourg City is a walking city. Everything is in fairly easy walking distance. Again Katy and I are going our separate ways, she to walk the city and I to drive to places I want to see.

If we want to change hotels, we have to check out of the Axe this noon. We agree to meet after our separate adventures.

My first visit will be to the military cemetery at Ham, just outside Luxembourg City. I drive up to the Petrusse Valley that marks off the old city and turn right onto Boulevard du General Patton, and down into one of the valleys. In a few miles, the signs to the American Military Cemetery appear, and I pull into an empty parking lot.

The parking lot is visually separated from the cemetery, by obvious design. A gate leads into the entry area, with a sign saying, "Respect and Silence" on the walkway, beneath the lintel that names the cemetery in gold letters.

The entry area is an enclosure maybe 50 yards across, with a shaft-like marble building, just large enough to hold a half dozen people in its chapel, in the middle. A high marble wall on the left of the entrance bears the names of Americans who died in the region and whose remains were not recovered.

Mosaic walls on either flank of the entry enclosure show maps of the movements of the units, one in Normandy and one over the whole of Europe. A line of red arrows marks the movement of the 537th (and associated units -- no one heard of us) from the beach to Linz, Austria.

Then, on a slope away from the enclosure, there stand the rows of white crosses and stars of David. There are thousands of them. Big American flags at permanent half-staff stand at either side.

And in the center, back against the viewing rail and facing "his men," is the solitary cross of George Patton. Even dead, that man …

As I am about to leave, a small group of Japanese tourists walks silently across the enclosure. When they have passed, I notice that they have left a wreath.

When the 537th was in Luxembourg, this cemetery did not exist. None of the men are of the 537th are buried here. But the effect is still strong.

Then I drive on through the edge of the town of Sandweiler, where the airport now stands. Part of our unit was stationed at Sandweiler.

1944: I think that it is at Sandweiler; if so, it is especially fitting that the event takes place where the airport will be in 1994.

I have taken hot chow to the men of our Company who are stationed at Sandweiler. An American P-47 fighter plane, its hydraulic system shot out and probably with other damage, makes a forced landing in a field across the road. With no hydraulics it can't lower its wheels to land, and comes in on its belly, plowing across the field and bending its propeller. The P-47 is a stubby, brutal plane, weighing nearly ten ton when fully armed and loaded. A lot of that weight is the radial motor, cranking out 2000 horsepower. It carries eight .50 caliber machine guns in its wings. It is made up of a motor, guns, and just enough plane to carry them and half a ton of bombs. Anyhow, this one comes in. The pilot walks away. The next day, a crew comes and jacks up the plane to lower its wheels, puts on a new propeller, patches what needs to be patched. Then the plane takes off and flies away. Tough customer.

Another incident, maybe at Sandweiler, maybe at Eschweiler, probably the latter. Some of us are billeted in an edge-of-town farm complex, the buildings surrounding a courtyard whose main feature is a neatly squared pile of manure in a stone-lined leaching pit (the liquid makes great fertilizer; the smell alone will revive a turnip). For fifty years, the image will persist in my retina, and will be clear as a photograph even now. The barn is behind me, the driveway to my left, and the house to the left beyond that, there are sheds to the right. I am being told that the Red Cross will not be able to get me home in time for Dad's funeral. I knew that he had had surgery for stomach cancer some time ago, but had thought that he had recovered. He had recovered well for a time but then had a pulmonary embolus. I don't get all those details in the message, essentially only being told that he had died. I decide not to go home, because if I do I won't rejoin the outfit and will become just another replacement, maybe in the Pacific. For all the hay that fiction writers will get about the Army's efforts to respond to family crises, in reality there is not much chance to interrupt a war for such reasons.

1994: Beyond Sandweiler I turn southward. This time I have a good map, and besides, I've been there before. I'm looking for Dalheim, the town where most of the 537th spent the time of The Bulge.

The map and a road sign agree at an intersection that Dalheim is to the right. This is, as far as I recall, the intersection where a German tank brought the

Bulge as close as it ever got to our quarters. The road winds back through a couple of smaller towns, then up onto the plateau. The red tile tops of houses appear over the edge of the plateau and the road drops down. Very quickly I am beside the house where Headquarters Platoon was housed for those weeks.

The house has been fixed up since Bernice and I visited it in 1987. Then, the walls showed cracks and spalled chunks around the windows, and the low wall along the sidewalk was fallen into disrepair. Now, though the patches show, the house walls are smooth and the low wall is straightened and new capstones crown it. I pull past it, and since there is no room to park otherwise, bring the car to rest beside someone's front door. I walk back up the incline.

1944: Dalheim is a farm town, though a big one. Cattle are kept in the farms that make up the outer edge of the town. We are scattered about the town, with Headquarters Platoon taking a sort of manor home, three stories high including a walkout basement where we can set up a completed kitchen.

1994: No one is about at any of the houses. I walk back to the driveway that slants sharply back and a bit downhill from the edge of "our" house's property line. A magnolia tree is in bloom beside the garden gate. No doubt the tree was there in 1944, but naturally it wouldn't be noticed in the winter.

There is the garden behind the house, a tree garden in the European manner. The garden was overgrown and untended in 1987. Now it is all neated up. The trees are different, as is to be expected after fifty years. The house looks prosperous. I take a few pictures.

Christmas Day, 1944. We have pretty decent rations now. Parker and I go to the ration point every day. It's at Esch, a large town near the French/Belgian border. In

104

the long span of our stay we get to be fixtures at the ration point. One day I take in, for trade, a large nickel plated German flagstaff head, an eagle with its wings spread about twelve inches over the wreathed swastika. The men at the ration depot are thrilled. In the then-mostly-segregated Army, they are "Negroes" who don't get any chance to pick up their own souvenirs. In return they give us a case of D rations, 24 four-ounce blocks of pure chocolate. Parker and I now have Europe's premier currency. Money is just paper, but chocolate on a continent that hasn't had any for some years will pay for almost anything.

Christmas dinner gets us special holiday rations, and Sgt. Hamilton and the kitchen crew prepare the goodies. But they lack something. My day's work is pretty well done when I've completed the ration run, so a couple of others and I are detailed to go out in the garden, where there is a new fall of pure snow. We gather buckets of it, and Hamilton transforms it with powdered milk and powdered eggs. We all have ice cream, somewhat grainy but wonderful.

1987, Bernice and I stop here and meet the woman who had owned the house in 1944 and who still owns it in 1987. She is fairly old, and speaks no English and little German, which is unusual in Luxembourg. We speak no French. With mixed languages, mostly German, we find out that she had turned the house over to the US Army, that we were the first users, and that several other units used it after us. She knows the names of all the units, including ours. By 1994 she is probably very old, and in 1987 she appeared to be alone and poor. At any rate, some one who is more hale and probably richer has fixed up the house now. (Kirstein had word that this woman was alive in the 1990s, so maybe she still is.)

Back out to the front of the house, where I can see "Cornell's chimney."

1944: We are going to be at Dalheim for more than a month while the Bulge is fought out just north of us. Bridge builders have no place in such a fight and we are simply put out of the way and left alone. Only in our last week or so in Dalheim will any of our men be involved directly.

We settle in and make the place as comfortable as we can. One problem is the chimney, which doesn't draw well. There are enough farm boys in the bunch to diagnose the problem as a chimney that needs cleaning.

How to do it? A good blast of air should do the trick. Cornell, who runs the air compressor, is persuaded to set up and pressurize the tank. Then a couple of the men take a hose in and point it up the chimney to blast out the soot.

Bad idea. The chimney is just like the ones of that era in this country. It has openings for stovepipes in all the rooms around it, and an unused opening is blocked by a steel disk with spring clips. The air is turned on, and pressure builds up in the chimney. The company commander, Captain Maraska, has a room with a covered stovepipe opening, and it doesn't stay covered. It blows out and all the soot in the world spews out into the room and all over the Captain and his belongings. For a fairly small man, Maraska can work up a towering rage.

At first sight, the overgrown trees in a cluster in front of the house (they were bushes in 1944) had concealed the statue of the nymph at the fountain. At second look, it's still there.

I walk along the sidewalk to the back of the house. Still no one around. Back on the street, I notice a man and a woman in the yard of a house down the street, the one with the rendolent manure pile.

1944: Just down the street from our manor home is one of the small in-town farms. Its courtyard is beside the street, and it has one of those neatly squared-off manure piles. Even in winter a good manure pile is "working," and it doesn't freeze. It keeps on steaming and it smells like -- well, like a pile of cow manure. The town is steeped in the aroma.

A couple of doors down is another house. The Luxembourgers are happy to see Americans, and the passion of their hatred of Germany will last for at least half a century. On Christmas Day, I'm visiting one of the homes, and we all must have a Christmas toast. I explain that I don't drink, but it's Christmas and there is no way to decline. The toast is in peppermint schnapps. I've seen this stuff (in another town) coming out of the still at 140 proof, 70% raw alcohol. This little glass burns a hole straight down to my stomach.

While we're at Dalheim we somehow get a radio, perhaps one that was left in the house. There is not much on the air in wartime but we do pick up the station at Malmö, in the south of Sweden. It's playing the Swedish version of the US Hit Parade and is a welcome voice from home. The songs are the great popular songs of the day in America, which even in the 1940s is the world leader in popular music -- songs like "Don't Sit under the Apple Tree," "In the Mood," and "The White Cliffs of Dover." However, they've been translated into Swedish. Songs are notoriously hard to translate faithfully, even though we have successfully translated many Swedish hymns into English, some of them quite true to the original (Example: "Children of the Heavenly Father," more accurately entitled "Security.") I know enough Swedish to realize that not all of the translations are very graceful.

One is introduced by the announcer as "Svinging on a Store (Star)." Not bad in Swedish, "Svingend' pa en Stjern." But they do have trouble with the inane English lyrics:

"... or would you rather be a pig?

A pig is an animal with dirt on his face,
His shoes are a terrible disgrace;

He's got no manners when he eats his food,
He's fat and lazy, and extremely rude;
But if you don't care a feather or a fig,
You may grow up to be a pig.

Or would you like to swing on a star,
Carry moonbeams home in a jar,
And be better off than you are—
Or would you rather be a mule?

A mule is an animal with long, funny ears ..."

Such lyrics are hard enough to explain in English. You can only guess what the Swedes must think about the depth of our nation's philosophy.

1994: I take one more picture, and when I turn to go and talk to the man and woman, they're gone. They were probably wondering who had parked a car and wandered off.

Time is getting away, and I must get back to rendezvous with Katy so that we can change our hotel.

Back in the city, Katy has had more success with way finding than she had in Metz. Luxembourg is a walking city. You can walk all over the main parts in a morning, if you move along. She has gone up the street by the train station and crossed the bridge over the Petrusse Valley, looking down on the stream and roadway far below and over to the bits of ancient fortification on the right. Then into the old city, past the cathedral and the souvenir stalls on the sidewalk, and back across the other main bridge. Now she's ready to move.

We have located a better hotel, the Delta. There is a parking ramp across the street from it, and we have earlier made arrangements and reserved a room. The desk clerk at the Axe doesn't even ask why we're moving on.

Odd fact: each of the hotels has a large, friendly dog that seems to live in the lobby.

We check in, and now both of us get into the car and head out on the road. Katy would like to see the cemetery, too, so we drop into the canyon via the Avenue General Patton and head out. The routine is a repeat of my visit in the morning.

Then we head north-northeast to Echternach. This is the point through which we all flowed after the Bulge was broken, and I want to show Katy the crossing point. Echternach is an old city on the Sauer River that divides Luxembourg from Germany. In 1944, the other side of the river was occupied by the West Wall, the Siegfried Line that was Germany's last defense, to be held at all costs.

1944: The finale of the Bulge is to be the crossing of the Sauer River, the border between Luxembourg and Germany. The thrust into the Saar Valley earlier was tentative; this one is to be the start of the real invasion of Germany.

There are only a few places where a modern army can invade around here. For a span of 100 miles of border, there are only two or three places where there is a combination of border-crossing roads and terrain on the other side that can support aggressive troop movement. Echternach is in the center of this. On the other side of the river, unlike the situation north and south, there are valleys that lead into Germany. The valley of the Mosel (to now use the German spelling) south of here is too twisted and narrow and too easily defended from its dozens of overlooks. At Echternach, the valley of the Prüm gives a fairly broad access with reasonable grades to the several roads that radiate out of there.

But the trouble with Echternach is that, on the other side of the Sauer River, which is only about 75 feet wide and about six feet deep, begins the Siegfried Line. This is Hitler's West Wall, the serious defense of Germany. The flats back from the river are mined. Just beyond that are the "dragon's teeth," the staggered rows of three to four foot high, flat topped concrete pyramids that are designed to strand tanks on their bellies. The land undulates back for three kilometers or so, and on every knoll is set a hardened bunker with light and heavy weapons. About three to five kilometers back is the line of bluffs, with bigger fortifications and weaponry set into the brow. This place is impregnable. We have to go through anyway.

For the past month we have occasionally seen trucks moving forward on the roads, towing trailers with genuine sea-going landing craft. These are intended for the Rhine crossings. We also have seen tanks moving up, with calliopes on top. A calliope is a bank of 60 six-inch rockets. What we haven't seen, but have heard rumored, is the proximity fuses for artillery: fuses that explode the shell when it comes within 40 feet of anything. The last two will play critical roles in the coming battle.

Once the Bulge has been pushed back to the Luxembourg/Germany border, Light Ponton Engineers are useful again. The crossing at Echternach will mostly use our assault boats and our two captured inboard powerboats, and our floating footbridges. The idea is to get infantry across to establish a bridgehead. Artillery support can be given from the Luxembourg side until the bridgehead gets too big.

The footbridges work, as do the assault boats. Getting the boats to the infantry is dangerous work. We get a few men wounded here, fortunately mostly minor wounds. Even the man whose power boat took a direct hit by an 88 (is it West?) is able to rejoin the outfit later. And one of our men, running up a flight of stone steps to get away from a burst from a German burp gun, gets a Purple Heart for the blister raised when a hot slug lodges in the heel of his shoe, and the gunner doesn't give him time to take the shoe off.

The street into town slopes down into the Sauer Valley, winding only a little. Then, in the heart of the old town, we come to the triangular square.

1944: After the crossing has been successfully forced, and the Siegfried Line has been breached so we can pour through, our whole Company drives through Echternach to cross over and head for Bitburg. The breakthrough has been sudden. In the town square of Echternach are still the bodies of our infantrymen, stacked in rows like cordwood. Echternach has been a costly crossing.

1994: Passing through the square, we find a parking spot against the wall near the police station, and take care of the parking meter. I mark out the historical museum across the street to be visited later. Right now our interest is in the rest rooms below it.

We walk back to the square and try a little shopping. Not much of interest, except for a really good bakery. Why can't American bakeries be as good as those in Europe? In a corner of the square is a restored older building, with a plaque that notes that here Charlemagne granted the charter to Echternach 1300 years ago.

1944: Once over the bridge on the Sauer (someone else built it), we can see the remains of the Siegfried Line.

Gaps have been blasted in the dragon's teeth. On many knolls, where pillboxes stood, there are only holes. This is the work of the calliopes, the tank-mounted banks of rockets. The pillboxes were too tough to knock out with conventional artillery and too hard to reach with hand-placed satchel charges. With a calliope, you zero in with the first couple of rockets and when you're on target, you fire off the rest in rapid succession. The cumulative effect crumbles the concrete.

As for the proximity fuses, also first used here, their effect is seen all over. The trees look like they have been mowed with a big lawn mower, their top sections shredded down to their trunks. And the shrapnel was so thick that the sheathed telephone cable that had hung beside the road is lying in 18-inch chunks, chopped up by flying steel.

Strange things are done by men who have already given themselves over to death. Fatalistic things. I can't vouch for the accuracy of this next report, but its credibility is enhanced by what I know of the disregard shown for booby traps in searching a house

Anyhow, across the Sauer River from Echternach is a flat area in front of the dragon's teeth tank traps, where any sensible defender would emplace anti-tank and anti-personnel mines. One of our platoons is detailed to help with the mine clearing. The report that comes back is that they got tired of probing carefully with their trench knives to locate buried mines, and stood up, linked arms, and trampled the field to locate anti-personnel mines. These would be Schuh mines, about a pound of TNT set to explode when stepped on. No Schuh mines. Then they took a truck and drove it all over the field to demonstrate that there were no anti-tank mines. These would be Teller mines, about 11 pounds of TNT. No Teller mines. Well, I can't vouch for the truth of this tale, but it's credible anyway.

> *I want Katy to see the German defenses, so we drive over the bridge into Germany and go some five kilometers to Irrel. Just at the far end of the town is the poorly marked road that leads up to the West Wall Museum, as they call it. The road winds steeply to the crest of the hill.*

> *We are at the Katzenkopf, the Cat's Head. This is a strong point, a concrete gun emplacement and command center that overlooks the valley of the Prüm. It has been restored into a memorial, a little city park. We get out and bring the lunch we had bought in the square. The pillbox is more restored than it was seven years ago when Bernice and I visited it. But the same memorial wreath stands on*

its bipod on the back of the rock against which the pillbox was built. The bronze plaques note that this is dedicated to the memory of the 35th Regiment Düsseldorf, and say, "Hier sterben sie (Here they died)." And it lists places that mark out the regiment's route through southeast Europe, the Bend of the Don in Russia, in front of Moscow. The list ends with the Ardennes, 1944-45. They lost 35,000 men. Well, at Echternach, we lost men, too.

Katy and I are finishing our lunch when two men walk up and sit on a park bench. I go over and talk to them. We discuss the battle here. One of the men was in Irrel when we came through. Both men are friendly. It's been 50 years.

We get in our car and drive back to Echternach. While Katy shops, I go to the museum. It's a curious place, the sort of thing that happens when a local antiquarian donates an adventitious collection to start a museum. There is a fairly well organized set of cases of stone tools and artifacts found in Luxembourg. This was evidently good hunting territory before the age of metal. There are metal artifacts, too, going up to the modern period. Also collections from Australia and other far points.

After I stop at my favorite hardware store to buy out their stock of those hook-bladed paring knives you can only get in Europe, I meet Katy and we go to look for the memorial stone that commemorates the liberation of the city. We find it down by the river, with its bronze plaque:

**IN GRATITUDE
TO THE VALIENT
SOLDIERS OF THE
83rd-4th and 5th US INF. DIVS.**
WHO LIBERATED THE CITY OF ECHTERNACH
OCT.-DEC.1944 AND TO THE
78TH U.S. INF. DIV

WHO CROSSED THE RIVER SAUEER HERE ON
FEB.-7-1945
ENDING THE NAZI OPPRESSION OF OUR
COUNTRY.
THE CITIZENS OF ECHTERNACH

Then, finished with Echternach, Katy and I move out. The ride back to Luxembourg City, half way across the country, takes a half hour.

Dinner. We look for a good restaurant, and settle for the restaurant-lounge of one of the main street hotels. The food is quite good. Katy looks above her, and there is a framed photograph. Eisenhower, Patton, and their aides are having 1944 Christmas dinner in this very room. We have eaten with history.

Our hotel is a great improvement over the Axe. We overlook a quiet interior courtyard.

(Then, in 1994, Katy and I drive through Belgium back to France and the plane ride home. But that story is elsewhere. In the next chapter, we pick up the German portion of our adventures.)

Germany

1944: We cross over at Echternach and into Germany. Another breakthrough, similar to the one at St. Lo, and the front becomes incoherent. The breakthrough of the West Wall, as the Germans now call the Siegfried Line, causes a tumbling pull-back of German units to the next defensive line, the Rhein River. Into this chaos we all pour.

Our road first goes northeast to Bitburg. I don't get to see the city, since the convoy turns southeast at the intersection short of Bitburg, but some men of the Company like Salisbury are on different schedules. They get to see the reduction of the city's defenses by the Army Air Corps.

(In this German portion of this narrative, "we" usually refers to Bernice and me in 1987. If the directions seem turned around, that's because in 1987 we looped up into German from Liechtenstein and Austria, and retraced the route backward from Passau to Luxembourg.)

1987: The road to Bitburg goes up the high hills. The roadway is greatly improved over what it was in 1945 when the 537th came down this road overlooking the bombed railyards of Trier. Then it is fairly straight on to Bitburg. Why is that name familiar? I'm reasonably sure that the 537th didn't go through this city, but there also seems to be more in the recesses of memory than the famous flap over the Presidential visit to the SS cemetery there. And it's clear from the map and the lay of the land that it would be difficult if not impossible to drive from Echternach to Trier over any other route, so this must be the road.

Bitburg, a mile away from the junction of the roads, shows a lot of US military presence. There are many cars with US military license plates, and the shops show a strong flavor of America. We park and walk around. On the Fussgängerstrasse (the Foot-Goer-Street or Pedestrian Street) we find an interesting bit of bronze statuary, a little cobblestone plaza with a half dozen life-sized little boys wearing goatskins with horns, down on their hands and knees and playing out some sort of masquerade that no doubt has a meaning we can't guess.

1945: Then there's open road across the highlands north of the deep Mosel valley. We crest the edge of the valley and turn to go down diagonally. Below we can see Trier. Its huge railyard is a shambles, all potholes and twisted rails and destroyed rolling stock. The Air Corps has made sure that this rail junction is inoperative. Some other Army units have come down the Mosel valley from Wasserbillig, a feat I would have thought, from the lay of the land, to be impossible because of the exposure of the winding road to retreating fire. The German Army must indeed be in full retreat.

We cross the river and go up the other side of the valley and onto the rough country in the triangle between the Saarland, the Mosel, and the Rhein (which makes a big S-curve to the east here). We pass through unremarkable towns. One bivouac area is near Bad Kreuznach. We angle around and end up a few miles back of the Rhein, opposite Mainz at Oppenheim.

1987: (Bernice and I cross the Saarland, an area that we didn't go into in 1945.) On a side road we find our first (and nearly only) bit of remaining WW II fortification, an overgrown and lichened section of dragon's teeth. These concrete pyramids, staggered and here only a couple of feet high, are designed to stop tanks by stranding them on their bellies with their treads off the ground, and when we went through here in 1945 the countryside was thickly strewn with them. We are 30 miles into Germany back from the West Wall, the Siegfried Line, and these are a last line of defense. But they are the only remaining fortifications visible to the traveler. The road is peaceful and there are no other scars of war.

1945: Now there is a pause while the Rhein crossing is contested. Fairly quickly, as soon as equipment can be brought up, the crossings are begun. The Rhein is too wide here for Bailey bridges, but one of our units does put up a Bailey over a channel that runs on the west of the main river. That Bailey will stand for fifty years.

The Rhein bridges are floating treadway bridges, somewhat like the ponton bridges we made in the US during basic training, but with steel treadways and able to bear tanks.

The Germans throw every last bit of their defenses against the crossings. At night the tracer displays are spectacular. We are too far back to see the river, but what goes up must come down. The spent .50 caliber machine gun bullets patter down on the adjoining field like hailstones. An ME-109 strafes near us, its automatic 20mm canon leaving green tracer streaks. But the real evidence of Germany's straits is that the bridges are attacked by even old Stukas. The Stuka is the original dive bomber, and it was a modern instrument of terror four years earlier. Now, it's not only outdated and ineffective with its little bomb and light armament, but when it ambles down in its bombing run it's so slow that it's a sitting duck for anti-aircraft guns. Its engine still makes that screaming whine when it dives, but technology has passed it by. By now, though, Germany has little else to throw at us from the air.

We cross the Rhein in daylight, when our Air Corps has unchallenged air superiority. The floating treadway bridge is long and it sways under our weight, but we're nothing compared to tanks. Out we come on the other side, into a forested area. And we encounter our first Autobahn.

This is the four-lane, divided highway between Frankfort and the south. Such a highway is unknown in America, where US 61 is still a two-lane road just wide enough for

117

trucks to meet if they're careful. We roll on in luxury, even seeing deer crossing signs. We head into Darmstadt, our first stop east of the Rhein, to bivouac.

Actually, we get billeted in houses. There is not much left to billet into. Earlier, 900 -- nine hundred! -- B-17s had been sent against either Frankfort or the ball bearing plants at Schweinfurt but had to turn back from the anti-aircraft fire. Their secondary target was Darmstadt, and they dumped there their entire load of Molotov breadbaskets. These are 1000-pound bombs packed with one-pound incendiary bomblets, rotating as they fall and scattering the bomblets to burn their thermite cores at over a thousand degrees. All that is left of Darmstadt is a ring of suburbs and the stone walls and chimneys of the city. In what used to be the city square stands the remains of an unrecognizable statue. A native says that no one, or almost no one, died in the raid, but that can't be true. The fire must have been like that of Dresden. Such a concentrated firestorm will kill as effectively as high explosives. A couple of spent, twisted breadbasket casings lie in the adjoining woods.

(We may have seen that raid, though probably not. While we were still in Eastern France, a flight of B-17s of about that size flew over on its way to Germany. It was a truly impressive sight to see the formation, covering essentially the whole sky, pass over. The day had been clear with just a hint of haze in the upper atmosphere. Each plane, however, laid down a contrail, that line of cloud that forms behind an aircraft if the atmospheric conditions are just right. When the formation had passed the entire sky was overcast with quite thick cloud, and it stayed that way the rest of the day. That was the only time I have ever seen a work of man effect a change in the weather at one pass.

(We were close enough to the front to see what happened when the formation of bombers crossed into Germany. From below, thin threads of white rocket exhaust rose straight up, but wavering as the air currents moved them. Vipers! These were German defensive, manned rocket ships, stubby little semi-airplanes perched on the noses of rocket housings. As they rose into the bomber formation, they each skidded into a flat turn and fired their rocket weapons. Then the rocket and its manned nose would separate and the nose section would parachute down. The rocket body and the rocket weapons that missed would fall back to earth, and I wouldn't like to be down there when they arrived. The Vipers couldn't have been very effective, because I didn't see a single hit. A formation of about a thousand bombers must be harder to miss than the proverbial barn door.)

The house where we are billeted is undamaged. The civilians are unceremoniously put out, and we move our gear in to sleep indoors for a change. Inconsiderate as all billeted soldiers, we search the houses. In one house, an Italian military carbine is found, contraband that the civilians were supposed to turn in. It becomes a souvenir, though not mine, and there's no more trouble. I find in the attic of our house a box of .25 cartridges. Just what I needed. I still have that little .25 Colt automatic, and I was down to a couple of cartridges. I also find a Zeiss box camera, but leave it. When you turn your house over to enemy soldiers, you can kiss your possessions goodbye. The technique is called "liberating" things, or "moonlight requisition."

We move on into Frankfort itself. Nothing remarkable there, we're getting used to ruined cities. But there is a bridge across the Main River, and the Germans would like it to disappear. We are right on the path between some airfield and that bridge.

The Germans bring out their new weapon, the Messerschmidt jet plane. There have been reports about it but none of us has seen a jet (except for that Glouchester Meteor I spotted in England, and I don't think anyone else noted it). Anyhow, suddenly at dusk a fighter-sized airplane whooshes in from the horizon, low

119

and faster than anything we've ever seen. There is no doubt as to what it is, but none of us can get to a machine gun in time to fire at it. It misses the bridge.

Next afternoon, I'm waiting, keeping close to my machine gun. Again the apparition on the horizon, overhead, and gone. I can't get to my gun even when I'm ready for it. This is a new factor in the war. (Hitler goofs. He insists on using the jet as a light bomber, when it clearly is unbeatable as an interceptor. It's a good thing for us that they have Hitler on their side.)

The next afternoon, there's a P-47 waiting upstairs in the clouds, and he dives on the jet. He can't catch it but he has an advantage: he can harry it, preventing it from getting to its airfield, until it runs out of its very limited fuel. Apparently the jet had to crash-land, because it doesn't come back.

The front moves again, and we convoy out of Frankfort to the northeast. Half a day later, we are in strange country.

I'm riding shotgun on the ration truck again, but now Helfman is driving. There is the usual wreckage of war along the road, and my scanning eye cruises it. There! on the step of a German 88! It's a Luger pistol. I yell at Helfman to stop, I bail out, and I go grab that pistol. A few of the men have P38 pistols, but only a very few have found Lugers. I hurriedly check the chamber; it isn't loaded.

I run back to the truck and get aboard. As we move on I look closer and find that the Luger has a very low serial number, #9944. It was made in 1911. This is a prize. Helfman wants to go halfies with me, and I get my back up and refuse. I found this one, and I'm going to keep it. When the prize is indivisible, my generous nature takes a hike. (Later, some shrewd trading gets me a holster for the Luger, and an extra clip. Its 9mm ammo is not hard to find. It will go home with me, properly registered with the FBI at import, under War Department Circular 155, Paragraph 4, Section 2.)

1987. Ahead lies the Rhön. When the 537th came through in 1945, this area was a puzzle. We had convoyed in from the Frankfort area. Then we hit a strange set of hills that made no geological sense to me. They showed no relationship to the local stream pattern or to the mountains of central Germany. The convoy hit the western edge and then climbed up through atypical valleys and over heights that were neither erosional nor upthrust, eventually reaching an unexpected elevation. Now, in 1987, the guidebooks tell us what it is: the remains of a vast extinct volcano. The area is called the Rhön and one of its uplands is the Wasserkuppe.

We drive up onto the Wasserkuppe, a rounded upland several miles across. From there we can see as far as the light haze allows.

Then we cross a broad, lower area and up onto the glider airport. There we watch light planes tow gliders into the air, and see the gliders sail along the updrafts of the Rhön. We shop for souvenirs, not finding any we want, and then walk toward the summit behind the shops and offices. The wind is persistent and cold, and we who are not dressed for it give up the walk part way.

1944: The 537th convoy winds up into this strange hill country, among trees and almost gloom. We bivouac there, and in a building I find a pair of "tank" binoculars. They're heavy, designed for mounting on the tank. Too powerful for holding steady in the hand also, twelve power. The objective lenses are 60 millimeters across. Into the duffel bag they go.

> *They got shipped home successfully, and were in demand for family bird watching. Then they get taken to Rainy Lake, are seen by some locals, and they disappear. Easy come, easy go. But I wish I still had them.*

On we go, to Meiningen. Since I'm now riding shotgun on the ration truck and/or the water truck, I don't get into any action like building bridges. However, nothing gels in my memory about the others bridging rivers, either.

Meiningen is not so badly beaten up by the war. Maybe it isn't important enough. Nice town, though. There is a huge fountain in the city center. (Later, when Germany is partitioned, Meiningen will be in the East Zone. No chance to visit it until the Wall comes down.)

About here, we are briefly billeted in a house that is somewhat apart, not jammed into a city. It has feather beds, a luxury that none of us has ever seen before. We treat the house fairly well. The woman whom we have displaced comes back and knocks on her own door. Enough of us understand German to know that she is looking for "der Schlüssel"—the house key. No problem.

We are embarrassed to be squatters in her home. But we poke about in it anyway. In a closet, I find a man's suit coat, and on its lapel is a Nazi Party membership pin. This is a rare find. Only a minority of Germans are Party members. Another souvenir.

Now our course is set more to the southeast. Next stop, Coburg. We don't stay very long here, but long enough for me to have a couple of memorable events.

There is a stream, and I wander off toward it. Roaming around, I find a German mobile artillery piece, sort of like a tank but open on top and dominated by a big gun. I climb up onto it and am about to ease myself down into the seat when I see the primacord. That's the fat cord that's used to link explosive charges. This thing is booby-trapped! I climb back down very carefully.

A shortcut back to the Company area takes me onto a little field, and I walk out toward the road. Then, because I have a habit of looking at the ground, I see a very thin wire, painted olive drab. I freeze in my footprints and look around. There are other wires. I'm in the middle of an S-mine field. How I've avoided setting off one of the mines, I don't know.

An S-mine is particularly nasty. It's buried just below the ground surface, with a side "chimney" poking through and topped by three prongs. To each of these prongs is tied a trip-wire. If you step on the prongs, or tug at a wire, or cut a wire, the mine goes off. A small charge shoots a can the size of a pop can into the air. Inside the can is a core of TNT, and surrounding that is a couple of layers of steel balls. The can is timed to explode when it's about six feet up. If you hear that "pop!" of the first charge, your only hope is to throw yourself flat and pray that the steel balls will all go sideways. But don't count on it.

So I very, very carefully walk out. Fatalism is a great defense, but when you can improve your odds, you do it.

1987: Coburg, our next destination, is not far. We don't really expect to find our 1945 site here, because we didn't stay long or in a recognizable spot. We saw the castle, the Coburger Veste (Fastness or Fortress, and in German, the "v" sounds like an "f.") from the outside, and this time we get to go inside.

Bernice and I approach the castle, looking up at it from moat level, and circle up to enter over the moat bridge and into the massive gate. Inside is a courtyard and what seems to be a whole village stacked up in a multistory heap of tan walls and red tile roofs. Small groups of German tourists, including groups of kids, are also going through the castle.

There are armaments display rooms, the first devoted to early models of firearms. In addition to matchlocks there are more ornate wheellocks than can be studied in one day. A few are two-shot, to be loaded with one charge on top of another and with two locks on the side. All the pistols and shoulder arms are engraved and inlaid. Other trophies include suits of armor for boar-hunting dogs and dozens of boar spears. A trussed (and stuffed) wild boar hangs from an ornate tripod just inside the door of the room.

Another room is more military. It displays the castle's defensive weapons, including the eight-foot "muskets" with forearm pegs to hook over the parapet and take the recoil, and with two-inch bores. There are five-foot, two handed swords for hacking at armor. Recognition! so that's where it came from! In 1945, in Kulmbach when the Germans were ordered to turn in their weapons, one room in the town hall was knee deep in knives and swords. One of the swords, too long to be sent home and therefore reluctantly not liberated, was identical to these. Being less of a Philistine at age 63, I'm glad now that I didn't take it.

A room of Coburg castle displays ten or more jousting sleighs. These are light, one-horse open sleighs with lances and lance rests. Idle nobility can hunt only part of the time.

Martin Luther spent some time in Coburg castle, too. A suite of rooms displays his memorabilia, such as his writing desk, used in 1530. Another famous resident was, of course, the consort of Queen Victoria, Albert of Saxe-Coburg, but he didn't leave much memorabilia.

Having seen what we want in the castle, we move on.

Now on to Kulmbach, a stolid town on the Roter Main (the Red branch of the Main) River.

We are billeted out of town, along the river. The Roter Main here is canalized, with stone banks and long straight stretches for navigation. It's only some fifty feet wide, but that's all that a barge needs in Europe.

1987: The 537th stayed in Kulmbach for at least a few days. Now when Bernice and I reach the town, it is dusk and it doesn't look familiar. The "town hall" is still there, of course. We circle the downtown a couple of times, then return to a hotel-restaurant we'd seen soon after entering the city.

124

Parking is going to be a problem. Behind the hotel, a man gestures us to park behind his Mercedes. He tries to talk to us in French, then in Platdeutsch or Low German, neither of which we can understand, but we finally get along somewhat in ordinary German or Hochdeutsch. He says we can stay behind his car until the middle of next morning, then he has to leave. He recommends the restaurant, and says that lots of locals eat here.

The hotel is small and we get a room that is reached through the dining room, but the room is comfortable. For supper, the pork schnitzel and the Frankerisch Würstteller are great. We repack our suitcases, while the sound of the live entertainment doesn't even penetrate our door.

1945: The farm family where we're billeted has rabbit hutches. Helfman is from New York and speaks quite a bit of Yiddish. Well, Yiddish is derived from Old High German, but it isn't identical to modern German. We get into a conversation with the farm wife. She tells us that Hitler had told everyone to raise rabbits for meat, one of the smart things he did. Now, the German words for "rabbits" and for "to hate" can be the same, depending on how they're used in the sentence. Helfman goes on about how Hitler may have hated these animals, but Americans love rabbits. He cuddles the rabbit and coos to it. The conversation goes nowhere and the woman gives up. I don't say anything. Helfman doesn't think much of Minnesota farm boys. Let him flounder.

The ration point is in the town and I get wind of what's in the town hall. So I wrangle a ride into town on time off and go into the hall. German civilians have been told to turn in all their weapons: guns, swords, and knives. The weapons have been assembled in the town hall, under not much surveillance. There is one room with rifles and shotguns strewn about, and pistols on the shelves. I pick up a pinfire revolver, one of those strange transitions between muzzle loaders and breech loaders.

Each cartridge has a pin sticking out of its base at right angles, and the hammer falls on that to fire the cartridge. I play with it a bit but decide that it isn't worth the effort to carry it about. But I do pick up a small sporting arm. It's a boy's gun, with a 9 mm shotgun barrel (smaller than a .410) on the right and a 6 mm rifle barrel (smaller than a .22) on the left. You select the barrel to fire by rotating the block that holds the firing pin. Beautifully made, its grace and lightness appeals to me. I also take a Spanish .32 caliber automatic pistol, learning only later that its hammer spring is broken. (On our later travels I make a new spring out of a packing box strap, and trade the pistol for a silver pocket watch.)

In another room, about 20 feet square, the floor is knee deep in knives and swords. At the time I don't know that the huge, five-foot sword is a museum piece, but I can't take it anyway because it's too big. I'm looking for one of those Luftwaffe officer's knives with the silver scabbard and cord, and with the disk pommel with its swastika. But the place has been picked over. Still, there are dozens of the Hitler Jugend knives, the sheath knife that is the equivalent of our Boy Scout knife. One of those would be a valuable souvenir in 50 years, but now I'm not clever enough to take one.

1987: After breakfast and after buying souvenir Kulmbacher mugs at the hotel we set out to find the nearby village where the 537th stayed in 1945. The town was near the Roter Main (Red Main) river, but no other clues come to mind.

We circle the back roads for an hour. There is nothing that looks familiar. On the other hand, we do get some great scenery. In the woods, the morning sun strikes radiating streamers of light through the forest canopy, sometimes spectacularly. We run across a small university town, Thurnan, with its look of the 17th century: cobblestones, split and narrow streets, soaring steeple, town square, and even a covered skyway over one street. But no sign of our 1945 billet.

Back in Kulmbach we pause at the monument to German war dead. The roll of local names spans nearly a century, from 1848. The pillar with its Maltese cross is flanked by four black slabs of names.

Unfortunately, by Kulmabch in 1945, all our moonlight requisitions have begun to total up. The trucks are jammed with souvenirs. The order comes down from the Captain that we have to jettison all extra baggage. The order is pretty rigorously enforced and I can only hide a few things. I have to get rid of not only the shotgun-rifle, but some other things. What hurts the most is the knife my father had made for me. At least I give it a decent burial. It now lies at the bottom of the Roter Main. It was not a practical weapon and I should have left it home, but I couldn't do that without hurting Dad's feelings. Now, since he is dead, I won't have to explain to him what happened to his gift. If only there had been a chance to send it home from Kulmbach.

From Kulmbach our route continues east to Bayreuth. For some reason we don't stop there, and turn southeast toward Cham. We start over the hump of the Bavarian Forest. We are on the edge of the ring of mountains that marks out the border of Czechoslovakia, and the ups and downs are drastic.

1987: Bernice and I roll on. We continue near the border, that of East Germany this time. We can sometimes see, to the north and east, glimpses of the watchtowers. When the road swings too close, or when there is a side road, there is a signpost:

"US Force Personnel HALT. 1 km to German Democratic Republic (East Germany). Do not proceed without Authorization."

The road westward still parallels the East German border. A high observation tower on the horizon leads us to Trappstadt, where the road dead-ends. The tower is labeled an "outlook" and appears to have no military significance. Tourists can walk up its stairs for a Mark, and we have no coins. But from what we've seen of it so far, East Germany looks just like West Germany. But in any case, we are not going to get to Meiningen.

Somewhere around here in the Bavarian hills someone liberates some vehicles. One is a small charcoal-fired truck with a round, upright "stove" on its right rear quadrant to generate gaseous fuel from charcoal. It gets discarded quickly. Then there is a Volkswagen, prototype of the beetle that will show up in the US in a few years. But this one shows the German materials shortage better than anything else. It doesn't have rubber tires, because there is no rubber. What it has is wheels of hard maple or beech blocks, mounted on short springs around the hub. Not a great vehicle. Last is a BMW motorcycle, with a four-cylinder flat opposed motor and a drive shaft. It's powerful and fast enough, but because of its motor placement, it precesses when you hit a bump – when the front wheel goes up, the machine wants to turn to the right.

We also liberate other things. Humans.

Between Cham and Regen, on the route south along the Czech border from Bayreuth to the Danube, we liberate a town that has a labor camp. In it are Baltic people, mostly Latvian but also some Poles. They haven't been living in a stockade but they've been slave labor anyway, working in some kind of factory. They are understandably glad to see us and they include us in their celebrations. Probably by looting local German homes they get assorted liquor. It's a wild night. Some of the women express their gratitude physcally. They are doubly glad to see us, because now they're going to have us between them and the Russians. When we move on they join the growing army of displaced persons (DPs) whose main ambition (unless they come from an area that won't be occupied by Russia) is to somehow get to America.

Our other liberations are less joyful. Near Cham we pass a concentration camp that has just been opened that day. The gates stand open and the inmates (those strong enough to walk) have not even waited to be fed. They only want to get out. So they totter out in their pale blue-and-gray striped uniforms of thin cloth, and get as far as they can. Some get only a short way before they fall and die in the ditches. They don't even look at us, they just trudge on and they won't go back into the camp. By morning more have died.

We bivouac nearby and have visitors. After supper we dump the leftovers out of our mess kits into garbage cans. I go to the garbage area afterwards, and there are two of the men fishing bits of food out of the slops. The kitchen crew makes them quit and sets them down at clean leftovers. They weren't going to ask for anything, probably having no hope that anyone would feed them. Concentration camps kill more than the body.

Somewhere else along the Bavarian Forest roads, riding in the ration truck, I pass another concentration camp. This one has been liberated for a couple of days but it hasn't been cleaned up. There is a rail line beside it and on some flatcars are stacked the bodies, naked skin and bone. Closed eyes, many years later, will show the scene undimmed.

1987: The Ostmarkstrasse follows the west crest of the Ills valley to Schonberg, making scenic loops and dips through forest country, the Bavarian Forest. We cross more uplands, and cross the little river at Regen, far upstream from Deggendorf.

Then we make a departure from the Strasse and cut right (north) toward the Czech border. The road becomes smaller and more hilly as we circle around the Grosser Arber, a huge low cone of a peak that rises above the surrounding mountains. It has a chair lift, the signs say, but we pass it up. We head

129

for the border town of Eisenstein. While there we get post cards and mail them to Czech friends and we pass the border guards at the Iron Curtain. It is a forbidding place, and we snap a picture without stopping as we pass fifty yards away. The guards pay no attention to us.

Our road now runs close to the border for some ways. We can see nothing different but the feeling is there. We turn back toward the main road near Lam and rejoin it at Mitach south of Cham, bypassing Vietach. The names of the towns are familiar—isn't Vietach where we had garbage can visitors from the liberated concentration camp? Today we turn westward at Cham, mentally judging how far we might get before nightfall.

1945: The terrain continues to be deeply hilly as we continue south. There are rivers down there and we're bridge builders, so that's where we're going. German resistance is practically non-existent. Everyone knows that the war is, for all practical purposes, over. The German Army only wants to let us past so we can get between them and the Russians. Gen. Patton is making noises like he's going to go after the Russians next, so all of us would not be surprised if we simply kept on fighting when Germany surrenders.

1987: Schwandorf and Schwarzenfeld show up on road signs. The countryside is much more developed, and a freeway now connects the two towns. Gone is the curve in the road we negotiated in the ration truck, uncertain of where the front line was, and where a memorably attractive girl sat like a Loreley. It's been a long time, and she's a grandmother now. (No, we didn't stop in 1945.) The freeway cuts north, the traffic whizzing along, then we turn toward Bayreuth, where we think we might stay tonight.

Somewhere along here we liberate a factory. It also uses foreign labor, and the workers are busily throwing out the factory's products: flags and medals. I get a Deutchen Mutter medal, an inch-and-a-half blue enamel and silver Maltese cross that I'm told is awarded for having eight children for the Fatherland. It goes into my growing souvenir collection. There is also a new German display flag, some 5 X 8 feet, red with swastika and eagle-with-wreath.

Riding shotgun on the ration truck and the water truck, as I do, continues to show me a broad swathe of country. Once in a while, off across a valley, we can see an Autobahn interchange standing where roads were planned to cross, a new kind of structure to us but one that will show up in US freeways in a few years. We have never seen a cloverleaf intersection before.

The water truck is actually a ¾ ton weapons carrier, that squat larger brother of the jeep. Its stability is remarkable. One morning, rounding a curve on a mountain road, we hit a patch of frost (this high up, it gets cold at night in early May) and skid off the road, on the inside of the curve. We land, sideways, on a steep slope and skid sideways on the grass. The weapons carrier doesn't roll. But I get a nasty bruise on my hip from the sudden stop.

On my birthday, May 13, we drive through a light and brief snowstorm.

The land suddenly slopes downhill as we proceed south, and we enter the valley of the Danube. We emerge, down a side valley, at Deggendorf.

This is an ancient settlement. Nearby, though we don't know it, are the remains of an Early Iron Age Celtic site, to be excavated 40 years later. We settle down for a few days, here where a deep river valley joins the Danube.

Shortly before we arrivea BAR man scores a memorable hit. The valley is a deep cleft in the hills, and Bed-check Charley uses it as a fairly safe passage along the front lines. (Charley, you recall, is any German spotter plane, a light one like a Piper Cub this time, which uses dusk as

131

the cover for a quick reconnaissance.) The BAR gunner is an infantryman who carries a Browning Automatic Rifle, a heavy rifle that can double as a machine gun. This man takes his position on the brow of the hill overlooking the valley, and when Bed-check Charlie comes by, he blasts the plane out of the air with one burst. War is not a sporting activity.

Also at Deggendorf, we have overrun a German military installation that trains snipers. Among the spoils are a couple of German military rifles, the Kar 98 (Karbine designed in 1898. The Germans are still using the equivalent of our Springfield of WWI, a bolt action 8 mm rifle. They do have a new semi-automatic similar to our M1 Garand, but we only capture one of them in all of Germany.) With the Kar 98s are .22 subcalibers. These are .22 caliber rifle barrels and bolts that slip inside the Kar 98 so that snipers can train with the less expensive .22 ammunition. Of the two subcalibers we liberate one has a bent barrel, but one of our men slides it into the Kar 98 anyway and finds that he can hit a six-inch rock at over 100 yards. Pretty impressive. I manage to keep the subcaliber that hasn't been bent, and eventually ship it home inside a Kar 98.

Increasingly, the war is degenerating into a mop-up of the flotsam that has washed along on the sagging wave of the German Army.

On to Passau. We convoy downstream along the Danube to the Drei Fluss Stadt, the "Three River City." At Passau, the Inn River joins the Danube, flowing north from the Munich area, and the Ills River joins from the north. At this point the Inn is almost as big as the Danube, so Passau has always been a sort of center for river navigation across southern Europe.

1987: The next few miles south of Passau lead through the same parklike forest that was there in 1945. The parking bays and the hiking trails are better developed than they were. There are no farms. Then we join the larger road into Passau.

The city has expanded southward and the area is light commercial and residential here. Then we drop down into the Old Town peninsula between the Danube and the Inn, and are busy just keeping on course and out of trouble in the crowded streets. The guidebooks recommend a tour of the Old Town, especially the cathedral, but they fail to mention the dearth of parking, so we keep going across the Danube and turn right, over the Ills River, and head downstream along the north bank of the Danube.

The riverside road has been upgraded. More work is being done on it, so there are bypasses and minor tieups. The road goes almost down to the water in places and parallels the railroad embankment along the edge of the hill.

Our first look at Passau in 1945 is cursory. We are now heading south along the Danube, and after a few miles we turn left onto a road that cuts up onto the high Bavarian Hills. We end up about ten miles beyond Passau, at a village called Wegscheid. Here we scatter out and get billeted, I in a house sort of outside the village, on the side toward nearby Czechoslovakia.

1987: The turnoff to Wegscheid goes to the left and up into the hills. Bernice and I climb and turn and rise into the mountains one or two thousand feet in the next five miles. Along the top for a ways, and there is Wegscheid. The town has grown and changed and it's quite modern looking. It still has the two-story Alpine-style houses, with balconies edged with red geraniums, on its outskirts. Where was it we stayed, where was it we were on the day the war ended? We can't find it. We do find a house that might possibly be it, but it seems to be on the wrong side of town and to not have the right fields around it. Well, it was somewhere in Wegscheid, anyway. We drive all around the town a couple of times, drawing curious stares from kids and a few adults, then we leave.

While we are at Wegscheid, I continue to ride shotgun on the ration truck, daily riding back to the ration point at Passau.

Then, suddenly but not unexpected, the war ends.

Refugees have been crossing over from Czechoslovakia on foot since we arrived. There are Russians behind them, but not very close. All the Russian effort has been sent to the resistance of Berlin, so no one is controlling the movement of people. The people want out, before Russia moves into the vacuum. They flow past in little groups, carrying nothing. We have liberated some German Army horses, complete with the military saddles that resemble US western gear. So we turn the horses over to the displaced persons, the DPs, and they happily ride off. They go to swell the ranks of what will become a several-year problem to Europe: what to do with people who don't want to go back into the Russian zone.

The day after the German surrender I ride the ration truck toward Passau. Out of a side road emerges a German (the Thirteenth?) Panzer Division with all its tanks. They had laid low there until we could get between them and the Russians, and they come clanking out to surrender to the first passing American vehicle, which turns out to be the ration truck on which I am riding shotgun. So we point them vaguely to the rear, and go on our way. Why didn't I have the presence of mind to at least accept the commander's sword? I assume he has one.

The end of the war reveals the extent to which the German Army has been avoiding us. To hide a whole Panzer division in the woods until the day after VE Day, when they could have wiped out all the Americans for miles around, indicates how much the Germans have changed from enemies to allies in the last few weeks. Americans are "us;" Russians are "them." For a couple of hundred miles back German troops have been laying low until we are past, and knowing that the war was lost, have been just waiting for the right time to surrender.

The local populace must have known about them. That maybe explains the startled looks Parker and I got when we drove into unfamiliar country in our searches for the ration point. They must have wondered, were the Americans here in enough force to invite surrender? At the time, Parker and I had interpreted the looks to mean that we were too far ahead and ought to turn back. But then, maybe we were.

1987: Today all roads look the same. We take a picture of the one that looks most like what is remembered, but the odds are against it.

Back in Passau we exit the bridge just inside the Old Town and look for a place to park. There are parking lots and ramps by the river, but they're all full. We cruise for a while, then give up.

2003, some 20 years later, Ruth (my second wife) and I are on a Danube cruise. We've passed Deggendorf and I stay on the boat while the rest of the group goes to Salzburg and we reunite at Passau. We do that long-delayed walking tour of the Inn/Danube peninsula. We see the Nazi assembly hall and the famous cathedral.

We also look across the Inn Rivers to the bank where a little boy once fell in and nearly drowned. Some misguided soul fished him out, and he grew up to change his name from Schickelgrüber to Hitler.

While some of us in the 537th are at Wegscheid other parts of the Company have continued down the Danube, into Austria, to the city of Linz. Thus, we are strung out over a thirty-mile area of chaos. The Company is reassembled at a half-way point, the town of Dommelstadt above the Inn River.

1987 -- Down the Inn from Munich: Our first search is for the manor home where the 537th was billeted for a couple of months in the summer of 1945. It should be on the west side of the Inn River, a few miles south of Passau. We get closer and closer to

Passau without seeing anything that might be it. Then we drive through the little town of Dommelstadt, and there it is on the right side of the road. We almost miss it, because it has naturally changed somewhat in 42 years. We park where I found the Pengö, the aluminum Hungarian coin that even in 1945 was worth some millions to the dollar.

The old cherry tree that bore so well in 1945 is still across the road. The open field that led to our shower tent is still open and carries a good crop of ripe corn. You can't quite see over it to where the shower tent stood, its water heater made of a radiator that Ron Cornell liberated in Passau, but you can see where the land falls away to the stream area where the fish pond stood. Maybe the pond is still there; we don't feel like walking into the farmer's land, since the local social climate is not so pro-American as is the Rheinland.

The manor home is just like it was, at least as far as can be seen, but it looks dead. The fence along the road bears a locked gate that leads to a driveway that is so overgrown as to advertise no admittance. The yard is an impenetrable thicket of brush and saplings, and through a somewhat open space I snap a picture. (Murphy's Law strikes. When we get home, that turns out to be the only blank frame in the camera. The one picture on the roll I really wanted, and it's blank.) A car fires up in back of the house and drives away through a back gate. That is the only sign of life in the compound. The road out here is narrow with almost no shoulder, and the traffic is building up around a blind curve, so we decide to move on.

1945: The men who come back from Linz have liberated 18 huge artillery spotter binoculars. These things weigh 13 pounds apiece and mount on heavy tripods with built-in compass, level, and D-handles for aiming. This is too much for the officers, ever on the watch for distraction.

The order comes to get rid of all of them. They get turned over to Natvig and me, to take to the Company dump in the woods. I rescue one set -- the tripod is too big to conceal -- and Natvig gets a monocular that someone has broken out of the housing. Mine goes into the bottom of my duffel bag and eventually it gets shipped home from Marseilles. The binoculars are the best I've ever seen, ten power and with 80 mm objectives. Their resolution is such that, even in dim light, you can see the legs on a fly 20 feet away. (They will later spend several years at my father-in-law's condo in Palm Beach, overlooking the fishing pier and deteriorating in the sun and salt humidity. In fifty years they will delaminate their lenses and strip the focus threads, but they're still impressive.)

Life at Dommelstadt for the two months immediately post-war is pleasant. We take time to fix things up. A tent with hot showers is set up across the road from our manor home. Cornell and a few others liberate a hot-water radiator from a damaged home in Passau, and with a fire under it the radiator produces as much hot water as we could wish. A little stream and fishponds are found, and a bit of ingenuity produces fishing tackle. I catch a few carp, the esteemed food fish of Europe, but I throw them back. The farmer who owns the pond gets really upset and he rails at me in his thick Bavarian accent. I explain that I'm not keeping them, just catching and returning them. In his guttural voice, he complains, "Du will'st alles Kaput machung!"

We are in the parklike forest preserve for which southern Germany is famous. The deer are those tiny roe deer and I set out to hunt one. I sit down in a deer blind beside a clearing, definitely a well-used hunting set-up. A deer walks out and stands broadside 50 feet away. I line up the German military rifle and fire. The military slug, humanely designed not to mushroom, slides right through the deer, which takes off. There is not even any blood. This kind of hunting is not going to work so I give up.

137

Strawberries are ripe. The wild strawberry of Europe, Eerdbären (earthberries) to the Germans, are larger than the US kind and even more tasty but just as hard to fill up on.

Our vacation at Dommelstadt draws to a close in August. The surrender of Germany has been neated up enough for Uncle Sam to pay attention to his scattered and now-idle soldiers. We are to be moved back out of Germany, to either take part in the remaining Pacific war or to do something else useful to that effort.

(We later find that our vacation has credited us with the occupation of Germany, and we will get medals to that effect in due time, well after the war is over.)

We load up and head our convoy up the Danube for a ways. Back through Deggendorf, then Regensberg. Inland, we truck through what is left of Nürenberg. The famous trials that will be held there have not yet been conceived. We drive through a city of desolation, the largest destroyed city we've seen. Unlike Darmstadt, Nürenberg was visited by high explosive bombs. It is in ruins.

> *2003: Ruth and I start our Danube cruise at Nürenburg. The city has been rebuilt. However, when we drive along some streets the older stonework, serving as the foundation to the restoration, still shows those high-impact scars of bullets and shrapnel. We also get to see the Old City and its citadel, which we had no idea of in 1945. We tour the courtroom in which the war criminals were tried.*

1945: Then to Heidelberg. We come in over the hill, drive along the riverside road, and over the bridge. A very few of us know of Heidelberg as the university town of "The Student Prince," and we don't spot the ruined castle that will be its biggest post-war attraction. We have seen a lot of ruins, and a ruined castle is not an attention-grabber for us.

1987:   (crossing the 1945 route) We rejoin the freeway toward Basel, and move right along with the traffic.   Well, with most of it after a while.   It is a foggy, misty day and we try to poke along at 100-120 km/hr.   In short order we are at Heidelberg and we turn off the freeway to visit this storied town.

The town itself is not remarkable, having been almost completely destroyed by the French in 1689 and rebuilt in humdrum style.   Now most famous as a university town, Heidelberg once was one of the major fortress towns of the Rheinland Palatinate before there was a Germany.   The old castle sits in ruin below the brow of the hill above the town.

We drive up the narrow and winding way that leads to the castle, up steep ramps that must have been brutal for horses in the days of cartage.   We emerge above the castle garden and park the car, paying our nominal fee to the attendant.   The castle itself will not be open to the public for another hour.

In the castle garden a 15-foot river god reclines in the fountain.   He looks like all river gods, and is a twin to the one in the atrium of the courthouse in Minneapolis.   The grounds are fairly well maintained and there is a great view over the city and the Neckar River bridges.   Down below is the riverside road along which the 537th convoyed on its way from Bavaria to southern France in late summer of 1945. The riverfront city is unchanged.

The castle is a ruin, though it still stands in most places to the height of five or six stories.   Whole sections have fallen away though, and in the rear the fallen wall reveals the arched interior structure and the eight foot thick stonework of some exterior walls. It has a certain amount of grandeur in its decay.

1945: We cross the Rhein at Ludwigshaven and re-enter France.   This is a totally different France from the one we saw to the north a few months ago.   It is less rural. We pass through Nancy, where some of us spent a week's leave during the lull a year ago, and on to Lyon. Then south along the Rhone River toward Marseilles.

Southern France

Down the Rhone Valley we convoy, swinging over to the east to cross the hills and into Marseilles.

This old city is all new to us. Few of us have heard of it but we will learn more as we live here. As we drive into the city from the northwest we see our first French pissoire. At a stone wall beside the street stands a man, relieving himself against a drain set in a quarter-circle wall that stands knee-to-shoulder height. This is an improvement in modesty over the men we see elsewhere, using the gutter without any shelter. (We will find that the downtown pissoires are still more modest, with four walls. But they also start at knee-height.)

Our local destination is ten miles west of the big city, at La Rove. Our bivouac is a level area among the almond trees and olives and we have big six-man canvas pyramid tents. This is the comfort of a somewhat permanent camp, with wooden buildings for the headquarters and mess hall.

The weather is mild, hot but not oppressive because of the low humidity. It is, in a word, southern France. We are right between the Riviera and the delta of the Rhone. Now that the European war is over, rules are relaxed. The uniform is "pants, and we'd like you to wear shoes." The sunshine and light breezes are constant. I acquire my first, and nearly my last, upper body tan.

Most of the company is set to work packing war materiel for shipment to the Pacific. At first it appears that we may go over there too, but after a month or so it's clear that we wouldn't get there in time. We're just as glad.

Using the Army's gift of packing materials, I send home my remaining souvenirs. The German artillery binoculars come out of the bottom of my duffel bag and go into a plywood box padded with a sleeve from my German snow trooper's coat. The rest of the coat goes home, too, and in each of the two pockets is a small French muzzle loading muff pistol, contraband for shipment but unnoticed. The German rifle with its subcaliber gets a sturdy plank box. I find that the rifle disassembles just short enough to be shipped. Everything arrives home safely, I will find, even the French MAS rifle I'd shipped earlier and whose box was splintered and tied around with rope somewhere en route.

Packing supplies for shipment introduces us to the first version of a product that will enrich our lives in the future: duck tape. Here, it's a fabric tape in rolls an inch wide, but even its OD color will be adopted by the civilian version first available after the war. At least war does contribute to technology. A liberated roll will go home with me and remain with me for all these years, occasionally giving up a few inches to be used when modern rolls are too wide.

We have time on our hands, now that we only work an eight hour day. Passes into town are generous. On some of our time off some of us wander the area around camp. One day, another man and I are walking a road a mile or two up in the hills, and a French family dining outdoors invites us to partake of their delicacy -- snails. We decline. We are not yet fully civilized.

Beside our camp is the end of the tunnel that carries the La Rove canal from the harbor of Marseilles to the La Bere lagoon near the mouth of the Rhone. The tunnel is some 40 feet wide and high, and in the tideless Mediterranean the water stays the same level all the time. This tunnel is an engineering masterpiece, boring under the bony dolomite hills for nearly ten miles. Once in a while, a small barge comes through. None of us ever goes into the tunnel.

We do go to the beach of the lagoon, La Bere, to swim. This shallow salt lake is joined to the sea through the tunnel and to the Rhone river at its western end by another canal. It is warm and pleasant on the beach but I have the misfortune to go swimming on a day after the wind has whipped up waves and shattered fleets of jellyfish. The water is full of live fragments of jellyfish, and they sting. Next day I am in my bunk with a raging fever, sick as a dog. Let other people go swimming.

Then comes some real Rest and Recreation. I get a ten-day pass to Nice on the Riviera. I board the train in Marseilles and chug along the coast, past the island of the Chateau d'If out in the bay and past the point of land that marks the beginning of the truly open Mediterranean Sea. We pass through Toulon, the former naval base. Through Antibes, along the open bay, and into Nice.

My room is in the Rulle Hotel, on the beach and beside the Jardine Albert. It overlooks the Jardine (Garden), a small park full of things like date palm trees. The hotel room has fittings I've never seen before, like a bidet. There is a real porcelain toilet, too. We have been living a crude life.

The beach at Nice is not sand. It is made of cobbles, water-worn rocks the size of your fist. The hotels have board walkways and beach chairs, because lying on the cobbles is no one's idea of fun in the sun. I see my first bikinis, and I approve.

Just offshore are the iron pilings of the casino that was there before the war, blown up because it gave too good cover for a possible sea invasion that never came. In the early morning a man emerges from the water wearing a snorkel mask and carrying a bucket. He shows me the octopus he has caught, apparently by hand, and lets me feel the suckers on the tentacles grip my arm.

The days at Nice are spent doing nothing. The only diversion besides rest is a bus trip to the perfume factory at Grasse. On the way we drive the Grand Corniche Road that Napoleon had built, and we pass inland from and above Monaco. The tiny princedom is off limits to US servicemen. But we do get to hear the ceremonial firing of the canon on the seawall at noon, and we can look down on the city. We are unaware that Coustou is down there experimenting with his aqualung, the first SCUBA gear.

At Grasse we buy the obligatory perfume, I choosing some Chanel No. 5 and a couple of wooden cubes with waxy solid perfume in them. In Nice again, I find some inexpensive jewelry: a green chrysophrase ring and a bracelet of tiger eye stones. I don't have a girl friend (at my age now of 21, I haven't ever had a date, much less a girl friend), but I have sisters.

It is a wrench, though, to have to go back to camp at La Rove.

Our kitchen help is hired civilian now, so no one has KP. But we have to eat, and I still ride shotgun on the ration truck. Every day Parker and I drive to Marseilles, up over the hills. We climb up out of the flats where we camp, into the buff colored rocks among the maquis, the scrub oak shrubbery. We drive through the little town of La Rove on top of the hills, past its tavern, and on to the edge of the Bay of Marseilles. As we approach the last ridge we dive into a short tunnel. We can see the blue and gray harbor, framed as in a picture, through the tunnel, which is only about a hundred feet long. Then we emerge right over the harbor bay, a couple of hundred feet up on a sheer cliff, and turn sharply left. Across the bay some five miles away is the harbor of Marseilles. The water between is that mottled lapis blue and malachite green that only the Mediterranean produces. Our road angles down the face of the cliff, over the mouth of the La Rove tunnel, and onto the short foreshore of the bay. On our left is a sulfurous factory, the maquis for a mile around blasted dead by the chemical emissions.

We continue around the bay, now along the harbor road. On our right is the outer harbor with ships riding at anchor. There are some piers and a fair number of one-man civilian fishing boats. One or two are always netting for bay scallops, through the oily black scum of the harbor. We are now in the city itself.

Then we approach the entrance to the Old Port of Marseilles. This is the much smaller bay, domesticated into a rectangle a quarter to a half mile long and a couple of hundred feet wide. Its entrance is guarded by a massive fort, built (I think) by the Venetians but probably based on more ancient fortifications. Just inside the Old Port stands one remaining tower of the former Transporteur Bridge, the bridge that carried a platform across the harbor like an industrial crane in lieu of a lift bridge.

On our left is the rubble that remains from the German's dynamiting of the Old Port settlement. That rabbit warren of ancient streets, going back to the founding Phoenicians in pre-Greek times, was too good a haven of the French underground. In an old harbor city like Marseilles, the Resistance was hard to distinguish from the criminal Apache. The Old Port settlement, with its interconnected buildings and its balconies meeting over the streets, had a reputation. No criminal who escaped in to the Old Port was ever caught. So the Germans blew it up.

We turn left, onto the beginning of the main street of Marseilles, the Rue Canbierre or Street of the Hemp. The street leads straight up from the harbor, through the downtown area, and up to the park. The street still bears the name it got when the Greeks (pre-Roman) plotted a path through the marijuana field. In those days hemp was mostly grown for its fiber, though it was also used for drug recreation and drug-induced sacred trance.

The Old Port on our right is lined with small fishing craft. It's a busy place, this spot that gave birth to one of Europe's oldest cities. We don't know it, but we drive over the ancient shore of the harbor, where rest a few rotting hulls of Bronze Age Greek ships.

Parker and I drive the ration truck over to the right, to the ration point at the base of the hill where stands the Cathedral du Notre Dame de la Garde. A funicular (cross between a cog railroad and an elevator) runs up to the area around the cathedral. From there you can see out over the sea for miles. Surmounting the cathedral is the statue of the Virgin Mary that has been a landmark for sailors for hundreds of years. There must have been some kind of mariners' sighting marker here for millennia.

We drive past the fish market. In this odoriferous square the fisher folk of Marseilles display their catches. By mid-morning, when we get there, the sun has cooked the fish juices richly. French people shopping here buy scallops and slurp the creatures off the half shell, the harbor liquids running down their chins.

The streets of Marseilles are old-time, crooked and narrow. We drive a 2 ½ ton truck. Once in a while I take the wheel.

There is only one way to approach a bottleneck between buildings: you aim for the middle and, when you get there, you exhale to squeeze through.

Intersections are a different form of amusement. The proper etiquette here is to blow your horn and gun the motor. He who honks first -- and loudest -- has right of way. We always get right of way. The horn of an Army truck is distinctive. In fact, there is a thriving black market for stolen truck horns.

Loaded up, we drive the truck back to camp. We often stop at the tavern at La Rove. I stay with the truck. A young lady comes out. (I think that Parker sends her for sport.) She is -- well, she's a working girl. Eighteen years old, she's the best looking girl I've seen in Europe, and pleasant. She speaks no English, I speak no French. She wants me to spend some time and money on her. Her hands are busy and expressive. I almost die of embarrassment, being a shy farm boy. When I don't buy, she asks, concerned, "Vou malad? (Are you sick?)" She pouts prettily.

(Later I learn that one or more of our men who did visit her praised her skill but required medical treatment for the residuals.)

We draw guard duty at La Rove, even though we don't draw KP. We are not allowed to have ammunition now but I carry the little .25 caliber automatic pistol in my pocket. There is no real danger out here at the camp, though.

In town, things are rougher. We have one or more truckloads of men in town on pass every night, and we are only one of dozens of military units in the area. I walk around alone in the dark, into any area of the city that seems interesting. I'm sensible. I smile at the people, some of whom are not used to seeing lone Americans in those sections of town, I walk a straight line, and I avoid the parked vehicles at the curb and the openings to the dark alleys and doorways. In the six months I'm there, I never have any trouble.

We hear occasional shots at night in Marseilles, but we're used to gunfire and pay no attention. Then we learn that the Army is losing about one man per night to the Apache, the local amoral outlaws. Most are taken by knife. An Apache can slide a knife into you, lifting the jacket so as not to get blood on the most valuable article of black market goods (OK, the shoes are more valuable than jackets). Wander alone, wobble like you're drunk, and above all insult the local honest women, and you're dead.

There are honest women in Marseilles. There are also reportedly 40,000 licensed prostitutes, ranging from the girl at La Rove to cheap hags near the harbor.

There is an election in Marseilles while we are there. We get our first clue about southern European elections when the town is made off limits for a few days.

Another time, we get an abrupt cancellation of passes. There is a contingent of French Senegalese soldiery barracked in town. They are tall, blue-black men with faces covered with ceremonial scars, and they carry Lee Enfield rifles with 18-inch bayonets fixed at all times. We hear that one of them suddenly goes berserk and sprays the street with a Sten gun. When his clip runs out his officer walks up to him, places his little .32 automatic against the man's belt buckle, and empties his clip. When word of that gets around everyone piles into the trucks and lights out for camp. Our last view of Marseilles that evening is a platoon of Senegalese marching in our direction, bayonets up.

Some moments are indelible. I am walking from my tent to the headquarters building, past the dried-up almond trees, facing the hills beyond the canal, when the news comes. The scene will be vivid all these years later.

The atomic bomb has been dropped. The first one.

That's it. The real end of the war. Sure, Germany had surrendered earlier. Now the surrender of Japan is inevitable. This is the real one, the final one. We are going home.

That night, I write a letter home.

> "However, chances of a furlough home have upped just a trifle with the introduction of the atom bomb. While it is too early to make predictions, my opinion is that it isn't all bluff. And I'd give a pretty to know how the atoms are detonated. Working on what I know of German experiments, my guess is that a chunk of U235 is subjected to the simultaneous effects of several Monroe charges arranged around it in a hollow sphere. The electrons just take off like scalded cats at an initial velocity of 186000 miles per second. The high-speed shock wave seems to be the destructive agent."

So much for the secrecy of the Manhattan Project, when a 21-year-old GI in Marseilles can figure out how the triggering mechanism of an atomic bomb works. In fairness it must be reported that the first bomb was not rigged that way. It was the second bomb whose detonation I have described. Still...

The second bomb is dropped, and Japan surrenders. End of war.

Our Company winds up its packing job and moves into the outskirts of Marseilles to await demobilization. We will not be discharged as a unit. Instead, return home will be individually scheduled, based on "points" for length of service, where served, dependents, and age. Our company is broken up and inactivated and I end up with a few others from the 537th who have similar point totals. We are in a different Engineer company. Because I can type a little, I become company clerk and type up personnel forms.

There is little memorable about the next month or so. Being closer to town, we can walk in on pass. Our comings and goings are not much noted and passes are no longer formal. The only image of the time that will endure is of me walking back to quarters along the port road at night, with my pocketknife open in my hand, edge upward. Nothing happens, though.

Now the time for shipment home comes closer, and we are moved out into a staging area on the hills above the city. We are back in canvas pyramid tents, and it is what passes for winter in southern France. For a while, it "passes," then winter comes in earnest.

The mistral hits. This is the wind that flows down the Rhone valley from northern Europe, a steady river of air that flows for days at an unremitting 25 miles an hour. Now we know why all the olive trees lean toward the southeast. This is the kind of wind that will drive you crazy. But our main interest is not in wind as such, but in the cold. Ten blankets are not enough to keep warm at night. This is sheer misery.

Then word comes that we are going to ship out, and the day is set. The day before Christmas.

Discharged!

The vision of going home is so strong that we don't pay any attention to the mechanics of getting on the ship and getting out of the harbor. We don't even notice the Chateau d'If as we pass it.

When I again notice my surroundings, we are steaming toward the Straits of Gibralter. We pass through the Straits at night, and I don't get to see anything.

We are on a converted Italian cruise liner, weighing a respectable 35,000 tons. It doesn't pitch and roll much until we hit some heavy swells, and then it pitches and rolls with a vengeance. Fortunately, I draw duty moving food supplies that are located exactly amidships and at the waterline, so I spend the days in the part of the ship that moves least. Maybe my genes would have forestalled seasickness anyway, but I'm glad not to find out. Most of the men don't eat much on the passage. The stern, when I go there to check things out, is rising and falling some thirty feet at a time.

In due time, we clear the Ambrose Lightship off New York, and steam into the Hudson in daylight. Off to our left is the Statue of Liberty, and the ship takes a noticeable list to the left as everyone lines the rails to see her. Most of us take a vow that, if she ever wants to see us again, she'll have to turn around.

More numb herding by the authorities in charge, and we offload and take trains for home.

My destination is Camp McCoy east of La Crosse, where I am processed for discharge on January 6, 1946. It is exactly two years and six months since I was sworn in. One of the functionaries asks, as is his duty, whether I want to sign up for Reserve duty. I laugh.

From Camp McCoy it is a short train ride through La Crosse to Red Wing. There, where it began, "what I did in the Great War" ends.

Looking Back

When I look back over those years, what do I conclude about the ordinary GI that I was?

The war was a shaping experience. All wars are life-altering for those who serve in them. Remember that all Americans, civilians as well, served in WWII in one way or another. The whole country was altered as a result, as historians point out. World War One had had a lesser effect, for one reason because the American participation was much briefer. It had a much smaller impact on the day-to-day lives of civilians and a smaller proportion of the young men served in active duty. World War Two lasted officially for over twice as long as One, and it seemed that every young man was in active service.

At any rate, I was one of those who were shaped by WWII. As the tired saw goes, I went in a boy and came out a man. Well, not a fully-finished man, but a lot different from the shy farm kid who left Fort Snelling that July day. Just under three years after that discharge I was a married householder.

I was not alone. Remember that I was ordinary, and therefore maybe I can be considered to be typical. Most of my fellow servicemen settled down quickly, too. Those of us who were fortunate - - and that was a lot of us - - used the GI Bill to get college degrees. Some used GI loans and other benefits.

As to the benefits of the service time itself, I think that I was a little different and got more out of it than most. It isn't only that I had an easier time than most. It was also that I saw more than most did. I was raised to be an acute observer and to take note of my surroundings. Add to that the store of information I carried with me from my youthful reading habit. So it meant more to me than to the others when we experienced new scenes and peoples. Recall that I was the only one who even cared to visit Stonehenge or noticed the Breton accent. Not to mention the fossil finds.

My account may seem bloodless for a war memoir. The 537th Engineers L. P. Co. was in a dangerous business, that of building bridges at times and in places that the enemy earnestly didn't want them built, and supplying assault boats and footbridges under the same conditions. In spite of that, our company has something like only a 10% casualty rate, counting deaths and injuries. This is a low casualty rate for a Light Ponton company.

The core of this narrative was written in the late 1960s under the title of "What Did You Do in the War, Daddy?" It was framed for the use of my four kids because, when they were young, they weren't interested in war stories (after all, just about everyone my age was a veteran, and commonness makes for poor thrills) and I was not in a reminiscing mood. I look at it now, and its bloodlessness strikes me also. Was I really that much a passive observer? Probably not, but I definitely was an observer.

Looking back, I see some things that were left out, probably because they didn't link up with anything. The dead German soldier with the right half of his head cleanly missing. The night sleeping on a cold concrete floor, with Benedict's heart rate dropping to 30 and my own heart skipping half the beats. The deep woods next to our bivouac on the Salisbury Plains, where I could go for a bit of solitude. The field somewhere in Germany where a group of German soldiers had surrendered and where I picked up the papers of one Werner Hemmerling, including his Feldbuch (ID and personal record book) and the picture of a girl who looked exactly like the one who came into the field with a basket of food, and whom I told that Werner had been captured.

The memories of garrulous old soldiers are endless.

www.ingramcontent.com/pod-product-compliance
Lightning Source LLC
Chambersburg PA
CBHW021111090426
42738CB00006B/601